MW00787813

SOCIAL CRISIS
PREACHING

Lewis W. Stewart

SOCIAL CRISIS PREACHING

The Lyman Beecher Lectures
1983

KELLY MILLER SMITH

ISBN 0-86554-246-5

Social Crisis Preaching
Copyright © 1984
Mercer University Press, Macon GA 31207
All rights reserved
Printed in the United States of America
Reprinted November 1984
Third printing, January 1987

The paper used in this publication meets
the minimum requirements of American National Standard
for Information Sciences—Permanence of Paper
for Printed Library Materials, ANSI Z39.48–1984.

Library of Congress Cataloging-in-Publication Data
Smith, Kelly Miller, 1920–1984

Social crisis preaching

(The Lyman Beecher lectures ; 1983)
Includes bibliographical references and index.
1. Preaching—Addresses, essays, lectures. I. Title.
II. Series.
BV4222.S64   1984   251   84-6656
ISBN 0-86554-246-5 (pbk. ; alk. paper)

CONTENTS

To Alice

ACKNOWLEDGMENTS

Over the years, I have discussed most of these ideas with my students at the Vanderbilt University Divinity School—ideas that have given shape to my ministry at First Baptist Church, Capitol Hill, which I have served as pastor for more than three decades. In its present form, this work comprised the 1983 Lyman Beecher Lectures at Yale Divinity School.

If I could be accurate in acknowledging all who contributed to the development of this study, there would be no space for such a listing. I must first thank Dean Leander Keck and his colleagues at the Yale Divinity School for providing me with the opportunity to share these ideas there. Professors Walter Harrelson and Herman Norton, colleagues at Vanderbilt Divinity School, were extremely helpful in the gathering and interpretation of certain data. Professor Robert Williams of the Vanderbilt Department of Philosophy was of assistance in the development of certain sections of this work. Dr. Sheron Randolph of Tennessee State University helped in organizing some of the data. Most of all, I am grateful for the valuable assistance provided by my friend and colleague, Professor Peter Paris. Professor Paris read the entire manuscript critically and offered valuable suggestions for its improvement.

Finally, I thank my secretary Mrs. Doris Hall for typing the manuscript in its various stages of development.

Kelly Miller Smith
February 1984

I
PURVIEW

*I trust . . . that I have made plain to you my own con-
viction that the work of the ministry must be concerned
with social questions.*

*. . . I trust that you can see that this social teaching is not
something outside of religion.*

WASHINGTON GLADDEN

The focus of these lectures is social crisis preaching. The audacious claim is made here that preaching, in spite of its fragility and other problems, is a viable means for addressing critical social issues. This claim is not only based upon its potential as rooted in the Christian faith, but upon its record and accomplishments as well. The procedure will be to take a cursory look at the territory to be traversed in the endeavor, to review perceptions of the issues involved in social crisis preaching, to view the task from the perspectives of history, the Bible and the Black experience and to consider proclamation of the social crisis conscious Word and its follow-up.

SOCIAL EMPHASIS
AMONG LYMAN BEECHER LECTURERS

The concern with social issues from within the context of the faith is no new interest of this distinguished lectureship. Edgar DeWitt Jones, in his survey of the Lyman Beecher lecturers from the inception to 1949, includes a group he labels "Prophets of Social Change." Those listed in that category included Washington Gladden, Henry Sloane Coffin, Charles David Williams, Francis John McConnell, Ernest Fremont Tittle, and Garfield Bromley Oxnam. Numerous other lecturers not so categorized, both during that period and afterwards, have expressed this concern in various ways.

Washington Gladden, in delivering the lectures in 1887, had as his theme *The Tools and the Man*. While this title does not necessarily suggest social content, the specific lecture titles make clear this emphasis. These included such topics as "Property and Land"; "Property in General"; "The Labor Question"; "Scientific Socialism"; and "Christian Socialism." When Gladden returned in 1902 to present again the Lyman Beecher lectures, he concluded with these words:

> I trust, my brethren, that I have made plain to you my own deep conviction that the work of the ministry must be concerned with social questions. I trust that you will find in your hearts a growing interest in these questions, and that you will be able to communicate that interest to the people to whom you are sent; to kindle in their hearts the enthusiasm of humanity and to guide them in their thoughts and labors for their fellow men. And I trust that you can see that this social teaching and social service is not something outside of religion. . . .[1]

Gladden, like other Social Gospel leaders made an important contribution to the understanding of the social content of the Christian gospel. (It must be remembered, however, that there was a basic fallacy in this movement as regards the racial issue. Attention will be given this point later in these lectures.)

Bishop G. Bromley Oxnam had as his general title *Preaching In A Revolutionary Age*. The matter and manner of preaching must be that of the prophet:

> It is the speech of the prophet that must be heard in the pulpit of the free. It must be the declaratory of the will of God: "Thus saith the Lord"—the affirmation of the moral law, the principles of conduct. It must be the speech of judgment: "Thou art the man." It must be the speech heralding the new day: "The Kingdom of God is at hand"; "Let justice roll on as a flood of waters, and righteousness like an unfailing stream."[2]

Charles D. Williams, who was a bishop in the Episcopal Church, delivered his lectures on *The Prophetic Ministry for Today*. Ernest Fre-

---

[1]Edgar DeWitt Jones, *The Royalty of the Pulpit* (New York: Harper and Brothers Publishers, 1951) 153.

[2]G. Bromley Oxnam, *Preaching in a Revolutionary Age* (Nashville TN: Abingdon-Cokesbury Press, 1944) 117.

mont Tittle, whom a Black colleague in the ministry called the most
Christian man of that day, had as his topic *Jesus After Nineteen Centu-
ries*. Henry Sloane Coffin presented his lectures on a theme appropriate to the times in which they were delivered—soon after World
War I: *In A Day of Social Rebuilding*. Francis John McConnell, a bishop
in the Methodist Church, had as his title *The Prophetic Ministry*. Other
lecturers have taken this dimension of the Christian faith into account. It was either a major thrust or a significant part of the emphasis. The present effort is an attempt to continue that emphasis with
particular attention to preaching as a function of the faith during
times of social crises. It is recognized that this emphasis is problematic
for many.

CHANGE, CRISES, AND RESPONSE

It has been said that Adam, upon being expelled from the Garden
of Eden, attempted to pacify Eve with the explanation: "You know,
these are times of social change and crisis; we must adjust." The point
that transcends historical accuracy is that the present era can claim
no uniqueness as an age of crisis. Every era is characterized by change
and with change comes the potential for crisis.

With change comes the struggle on the part of resisters either to
maintain the status quo or to avoid the undertow of change. Sometimes crises are precipitated when there is considerable agitation for
change on the part of the oppressed, especially when this agitation is
met with obdurate resistance. Of course, crises also exist when there
is passive acquiescence on the part of social victims.

It may be said, then, that crisis comes not only when normal
change occurs but also when there is effort to effect change and when
there is glaring unmet need. In short, it may be said that the very dynamics of existential experiences keep some segments of humankind
engaged in seeking ways of addressing crises creatively. This is a perennial occupation.

There is a multitude of ways of responding to crises. Some respond through aggressive, constructive action; some through aggressive, destructive action; some through a nebulous "wait and see"
disposition; some pretend the crises do not exist and therefore do
nothing, and there are some who accept the terms of the crises and

engage in the behavior consistent with acceptance. Social crises plunge some persons into depression and despair while they may well give momentum and zeal to others. The pendulum can swing either in the direction of hope, due to such factors as the nature of the situation, the type and quality of action taken and the fruits of religious faith, or in the direction of abject despair and a sense of futility.

The response from within the context of the Christian faith will determine, in large measure, the type of action to be taken as well as whether there ensues a sense of hope or futility. It is clear, however, that all who contend that they respond from within the faith do not have the same perspectives on the meaning of that faith nor its requirement and promise in such situations. Actually, responses from within the faith may be as divergent as responses from without that faith.

Divergent responses to social reality give a rhythm to history. It is in a measure a rhythm created by the alternation of crisis and response. For example, three years after Rome was sacked that incomparable North African scholar, St. Augustine, wrote *The City of God*. When the transitional movement in Europe between the medieval and modern times called the Renaissance began to dispel the shadows of the Dark Ages, Campinella, responding to the times, wrote *The City of the Sun*. John Milton was responding to certain events in history when he wrote *Paradise Lost* and *Paradise Regained*. John Calvin was responding to the moral and physical devastation wrought by the Thirty Years' War when he set out to bring into being a city of God— not in a book, but in a city. Nat Turner, Denmark Vesey, and Gabriel Prosser were responding to the indescribable evils of slavery when they organized insurrections to change the course of history. Richard Allen, Absalom Jones, and William White were responding to the prostitution of religion when they walked out of the segregationist St. George's Methodist Church in Philadelphia, Pennsylvania, in the late eighteenth century and started what became the African Methodist Episcopal Church. There is an alternating rhythm to history formed by crises and their responses. There is always someone who stands up and says, "These things ought not so to be." Sometimes the respondent is a prophet who comes without "respectable" credentials, but who speaks to the issues and sets a new course for history.

Often it is one who has ascended the weather-beaten sides of the Sinai of his or her own experiences who declares, "Thus saith the Lord!"

The present task is to explore some factors involved in addressing social crises from within the context of the Christian faith. More specifically, the concern here is with Christian proclamation—*preaching*—in times and circumstances of social crisis. There was a time in human history when the human individual was considered to be helpless with regard to changing or even affecting the social order apart from conformity to perceived sacred tradition. Human beings were conceived as subject to the whims of a sometimes capricious but sovereign cosmological order. In the history of humankind, it is relatively recent that the human individual has been seen as a shaper of society and a maker of human history. The question is how this may be effected. When the suggestion is made that it may, in part, be accomplished through preaching, the reaction is likely to be one of amazement and perhaps amusement at such naiveté. This, however, is precisely the contention being made here.

RELIGION AND SOCIAL CRISES

It is clear that from the time of the primitive human family to the present, religion has been prominently involved in the effort to deal with crises. While this theme will claim a considerable part of the present work later, at least three observations should be made here.

(1) Close to the genesis of most religions may be found some circumstance—or legend—involving critical social concerns. For example, in the early conceptual stage of Buddhism, Gautama Buddha is said to have been influenced by a graphic picture of deserted and miserable old age, of painful, unattended illness, and of premature death. Of Buddhism, Taoism, Judaism, Christianity, and Islam, Vitorrio Lantinari wrote, ". . . these great religions began as a prophetic movement of renewal stimulated by certain given cultural and social conditions in a time of crisis."[3]

(2) No serious observation of a religious phenomenon is possible apart from its cultural and social context. How a religion relates to the

---

[3]Vitorrio Lantinari, *The Religions of the Oppressed* (New York: Mentor Books, 1965) vii.

"secular" is vital for the understanding of that religion. This has no reference to whether or not a religion has "worldly" things on its agenda. The fact is that all religions are "worldly" by virtue of their interaction with their social context. Lantinari observes that

> Premonitory religious movements of revival and transformation usually lie at the origin of every political or military uprising among the native peoples and take the form of messianic cults promising liberation.[4]

Acknowledged or unacknowledged, the interaction between religious phenomena and the social cultural context is evident. Paul Tillich makes this point more graphically in the observation, "religion is the substance of culture, culture is the form of religion."[5]

(3) Since the primitive era, members of the human family have addressed critical social concerns in religious ways. Primitive persons often worshiped, deified or in some manner gave special regard to that which could not be fully understood or controlled. During all eras social victims have looked to religion for relief. Sometimes they have called on the gods of religion and there have been times when religion provided the setting for the development of strategies to effect desired change.

CHRISTIANITY AND SOCIAL CRISES

The social relevance of Christianity is axiomatic. As is the case of any other entity, the Christian faith interacts with its social context. The question that continues as an item of concern has to do with the nature of that relevance. The perspective of these lectures is that there is a Christian imperative that requires adherents of the Christian faith to initiate action regarding social conditions.

The Judaistic heritage is clearly cognizant of social reality and it addresses that reality in many ways. Through the proclamations of the prophets, through history and poetry Judaism addresses social concerns. From its inception Christianity has concerned itself with social problems. The coming of Jesus and his words and ministry had

---

[4]Ibid., 19.

[5]Paul Tillich, *Theology of Culture* (New York: Oxford University Press, 1968) 42.

profound social and political meaning. The apostles were fully aware of the social and political implications of their work.

A vital characteristic of Christianity is its special interest in the oppressed. Not only is this concern inherited from Judaism; it manifests itself in the words and deeds of Jesus. This faith at its highest and best has a pronounced bias in the direction of the oppressed.

This realization does not entail an instrumental employment of the Christian faith. Its emphasis is upon truth rather than upon utility. It is this truth—this coming to terms with reality concerning one's self—that makes one free (John 8:32). The personification of this truth and the channel of this freedom is the central figure of the Christian faith—Jesus of Nazareth. This faith, in its authentic manifestation, envisions a just society made so by faithful adherence to the mandates of the faith. This means acceptance of the biblical dictum to seek first the Kingdom of God and "all these things" will be added. This does not mean that one should seek the Kingdom for the sake of "all these things" which will be added. Rather, it is to seek the Kingdom because it is a Kingdom of truth and because one's "chief end is to glorify God and enjoy him forever." "These things" are not added by magic, but by the productive behavior of adherents to the faith together with understanding with Martin Luther that

> Did we in our own strength confide,
> Our striving would be losing,
> Were not the right man on our side,
> The man of God's own choosing.

The Black church in America was called into being as a response to adverse social circumstances and crises. It became clear immediately that there was no discontinuity between the evil in White society generally and the social evil that manifested itself in the churches. It was in response to this experience that the Black church came into being. It was to provide opportunity for the free and full expression of religion—which for the transplanted African was not separate from the rest of life. The Black church did and does facilitate Black people's search for truth about themselves. The Christian faith transfers Blacks from the status of nonpersons to the level of somebodiness. This occurs not only because it is the chief resource available to Black people, but also because this kind of concern is the very heart of that faith. This is not an instrumental use of the Christian faith; it is an involvement with the very essence and substance of that faith.

SOCIAL CRISIS PREACHING

Although there is still lively debate in some quarters over the appropriateness of responding to social crises from within the Christian faith and over the manner and content of such response, experience shows that that faith is a major resource for addressing social crises. There have always been those within the faith whose agendas are formed as response to social crises.

The concern here is with Christian proclamation during times of social stress or upheaval. Admittedly, the territory to be covered in this venturesome journey is vast and foreboding. It is made so, on the one hand, by those who contend that this is not the proper turf for preachers and, on the other hand, by those who seek to occupy the territory themselves for the cause either of recalcitrant conservatism or lethargic liberalism. To traverse here is to risk the explosion of emotional land mines with which the territory is laden. While ignorance is an especially dangerous state under such conditions, it must be faced that the precise danger points are not in view. For the present, there must be contentment with the location of regions of the terrain that have the possibility of encompassing problem areas.

PREACHER VERSUS PERSON

It is interesting, and in some ways baffling, that some who have expressed themselves on this issue assert that the preacher *as citizen* may appropriately participate creatively and constructively in socially critical situations but, *as preacher* must not do so. When the preacher dares to function in this area, he or she is seen as a social activist or civil rights leader or peace activist. This type of thinking may well be more widespread than is generally recognized. For example, the U.S. press refers to Dr. Martin Luther King, Jr. as a "slain civil rights leader." What a tragic assault on the proper functioning of the prophet! What a diminution of a great name! What a flight from reality! Even more tragic is the fact that so many both within and without the ministerial craft accept this designation of King without protest or question, although its implications are ominous.

The "slain civil rights leader" designation says that King may have functioned as a preacher at times, but when he was immersed in the activities that pertained to human rights, that for which he is best known, he was outside the ministerial vocation. The appellation contradicts the major thrust of King's ministry. His work was an acting out of his understanding of the social content of the Christian gospel. Further, this was part of his impact upon the ecclesiastical community. Because of this preaching and his work a broader concept of ministry emerged. It was King who inspired ministers of all faiths and ethnic backgrounds to understand that there are times when marching in the streets and protesting injustice in whatever arena are continuous with, not separate from or contradictory to, the pulpit ministry. It is not too farfetched to suggest that the social awareness that expressed itself in some local churches, theological seminaries, and in the various denominations during the sixties in particular was influenced by the ministry of Martin Luther King, Jr.

Martin King was no slain civil rights leader; he was a martyred prophet of God who was killed for doing what prophets do. Social crises are precisely where Christian ministers should be found. The work of interpreting and rectifying wrongs in this area is the proper work of those who proclaim the Christian gospel. The words "social crises" and "preaching" do belong together. As a matter of fact, the term "preaching" in its most profound meaning *includes* a concern with social crises.

THE FRAGILE INSTRUMENT

Some are apprehensive about the notion of social crisis preaching, not because they conceive it to be an inappropriate area for ministers, but because they feel that the preaching task itself is grossly incapable of serving a useful function in times of social crisis or upheaval. It is a fragile instrument for so vital a responsibility. According to this view preachers may adorn clerical garb and participate in marches, serve as leaders of movements, address protesters, serve as negotiators, and otherwise function fully in socially critical times, but they must not assign importance to preaching as part of that witness. Preaching, as they see it, is perhaps the poorest way to address social issues and concerns—especially when emotions are high and immediate action is warranted. Some would apply W. E. Sangster's comment on evangelism and social crises here: It is like trying to sell a long-term endowment policy to one sitting on a time bomb!

The preaching task itself is called into question regarding its capacity to move beyond what C. Wright Mills referred to as "irrelevant Sunday chatter." Any who have heard the profound and eloquent preaching of Gardner C. Taylor would never think that he would call the preaching enterprise into question at any point. Yet, in his presentation of the 1976 Lyman Beecher lectures he referred to the "gnawing uncertainty about the value and worth of preaching which will doubtless afflict all of us from time to time. For one, I confess that preaching has often seemed to me such a clumsy and unclear form of communication. At its lowest elevations it seems many times to be a dull and unexciting rehashing of old matters."[6] George Bernard Shaw is reported to have given this commentary on preaching: "Some is like coffee, stimulates but does not nourish; some is like wine, has sparkle but no lasting value; some is like seltzer water, a big fuss over nothing; and some is like spring water—good, but hard to get!" Preaching of the coffee, wine, and seltzer water variety is what seems to be offered most of the time. How, then, can an enterprise so fragile as preaching serve as a viable vehicle for the resolution of social crises? This question must not be taken lightly.

While no claims are made here that preaching is the only way to approach critical social issues, the perspective of these lectures is that it is a valid channel for the expression of social concerns and, in spite of all its liabilities, it can be an effective means of moving people to social action.

QUALITY

The basic issue in social crisis preaching is quality. It is neither homiletical gimmickry nor general congregational disinterest. The

---

[6]Gardner C. Taylor, *How Shall They Preach* (Elgin IL: Progressive Baptist Publishing House, 1977) 42.

proclamation of the Christian gospel on the highest order will of necessity include the social dimension. Clever word manipulation and structural artistry do not equal quality preaching. In response to the issue of congregational disinterest, Paul Althaus has said that people are not tired of preaching; they are tired of *our* preaching. John Killinger, addressing the same concern, suggested that the people are not tired of preaching; they are tired of non-preaching. They are weary of "the badly garbled, anachronistic, irrelevant drivel which has in so many places passed for preaching because there was no real preaching to measure it against."[7] It may be validly charged that Althaus and Killinger thus give too much credence to the ability of the people to decide upon the quality of a sermon. The claim is being made here that some sermons that earn this negative assessment lack quality because of the absence of that which, to use a phrase employed by Elijah Mays and Joseph Nicholson, "touches life situations."[8]

The presence of this social element in preaching does not in any way guarantee large, enthusiastic audiences. To the contrary, listeners are often hostile towards that preaching that is prophetic and socially relevant. They may, indeed, become weary of social crisis preaching precisely because it not only comforts the disturbed, but it disturbs the comfortable. Congregational reception is an important consideration for the preacher, but is not determinative of the quality of preaching. That is determined by faithfulness to the Word and to the calling.

The issue is quality. Quality preaching takes into account that social concerns are at the very heart of the Christian gospel. In a measure, preaching is authenticated by the extent to which the social dimension is taken into account. More important even than this, however, is that the Christian gospel champions the cause of the oppressed. "The gospel is the proclamation of God's liberation as revealed in the event of Jesus and the outpouring of the Holy Spirit.

---

[7]John Killinger, *The Centrality of Preaching in the Total Task of the Ministry* (Waco TX: Word Books, 1969) 21.

[8]See Benjamin Elijah Mays and Joseph William Nicholson, *The Negro's Church* (New York: Negro Universities Press, 1933) 58ff.

... To preach the gospel today means confronting the world with the reality of Christian freedom."[9] C. Wright Mills says it more crassly and less theologically: "If you do not get the church into politics, you cannot confront evil and you cannot work for good. You will be a subordinate amusement and a political satrap of whatever is going. You will be the great Christian joke."[10] Cone, however, is concerned with faithfulness to the Christian gospel. His is an interpretation of the Christian imperative from within the faith. While Mills's comment feigns a concern with gospel imperative, it is actually concerned with the resource that the church represents, for Mills himself stood outside that faith. Both call attention to the social and political relevance of the Christian gospel. The thrust here, however, is the contention that this kind of concern is the essence of the gospel and that gospel cannot be proclaimed accurately without this emphasis. The Word of God "preaches" best when it is seen in relation to its function of liberating the oppressed. To avoid this emphasis is to fabricate a gospel that is alien to the faith that has been proclaimed by the most perceptive and faithful of the spiritual ancestors and is alien to the religion of Jesus.[11]

VOICE VERSUS ECHO

There are those who accept the notion that preachers may function in this area, but only insofar as they abide by the "guidelines." The term "guidelines" is used here to connote that which does not always have the force of a legal arrangement, but which can at times function in this way. These often include treading gingerly as if in alien territory when on the side of justice and peace and walking boldly when espousing the life-denying positions of social conservatism or conservative liberalism. The guidelines are often devel-

---

[9]James H. Cone, *A Black Theology of Liberation* (Philadelphia: J. B. Lippincott Company, 1970) 230-31.

[10]C. Wright Mills, *The Causes of World War Three* (New York: Simon and Schuster, 1958) 155.

[11]It is essential to distinguish between the religion *of* Jesus and the religion *about* Jesus. The latter may well include the evasions and misconstructions that avoid the social emphasis, but not the former.

oped and rigidly enforced by the unholy alliance of expediency and aggressive ignorance. In some instances certain members of the congregation expect (require?) their clergy to reflect the attitude of the congregation rather than to fulfill the prophetic function that is properly theirs. They are expected to be—not a prophetic voice, but a pathetic echo. They thus give meaning to the observation Kyle Haselden made: the church is often our culture having a polite conversation with itself.

Let it be understood, however, that adherence to the guidelines of conservatism or conservative liberalism has never characterized all of the spokespersons for the faith. There has never been a period of intense social crisis when at least some part of the church did not proclaim the prophetic word. The flaming and insistent words of the ancient prophets of the Bible are well known. Perhaps less well known are the prophetic utterances of the slave preachers and their descendants. James H. Cone makes the bold claim: "The Black church is the only church in America which remained recognizably Christian during the pre-Civil War days."[12] Central to this characterization of the early Black church is the proclamation of the Christian gospel. These proclamations on the part of the slave preachers were obviously done in an atmosphere of danger because the regulations had indeed been set. In some of the slave states rigidly enforced laws had been enacted forbidding slaves from gathering for worship without the presence of someone who represented the interests of the slavemaster. It was when these laws were defied that slave insurrections followed spirited services of worship and fiery proclamations of the Word.

Preachers in contemporary Black churches are not subjected to the same restrictive monitoring as their White counterparts. Black congregations, generally, establish no guidelines to restrict the social ministry of their pastors. Rather, in many instances, congregations expect their pastor to take leadership in these matters. As has been indicated, this is part of the reason for the existence of the Black church in the first place.

---

[12]James H. Cone, *Black Theology and Black Power* (New York: The Seabury Press, 1969) 103.

Marcus Boulware makes this factual observation regarding the
leadership of Black ministers during the civil rights era of the sixties:

> [The Black Church's] leadership, meanwhile has become bold, and the min-
> isters are forming civil-rights armies that are unsurpassed in dedication and
> fervor. Like four-star generals, many pastors have rushed to the battlefront,
> wherever it may be. As a consequence, for example, thirty-eight Negro
> churches were destroyed by fire in 1964.[13]

When there are guidelines to which the Black preacher is subjected, they are generally set either by those external and hostile to
the Black community or by a small majority within that community
who have internalized their oppression.

THE BRAZEN UNDERTAKING

Gardner C. Taylor places emphasis upon the presumptuousness
of preaching. Preaching is a brazen and audacious undertaking.
When this fact is fully understood and accepted, the inclusion of the
social emphasis becomes more congruous.

Logically, what right has a sinful woman or man to stand before
other sinful women and men for the express purpose of telling them
about their sinfulness? What really qualifies one, as Jeremiah, to be
"set over nations and over kingdoms, and to pluck up and to break
down, to destroy and to overthrow. . . ." (Jeremiah 1:10 RSV) when
one is not appointed by that structure to govern it in any manner
whatsoever? What *is* this madness—this unmitigated gall—that
causes one to speak when not invited to do so and even when forbid-
den to speak (e.g., Acts 4:18), to act when the people want none of it
and to judge with no certified credentials? The preacher is so woven
into the fabric of the society upon which the critical judgment is made
that he or she must keep the prayer of the ancient psalmist upon his
or her lips: "But who can discern one's own errors? Clear thou me
from hidden faults. Keep back thy servant from presumptions sins;
let them not have dominion over me!" (Psalms 19:12, 13 RSV). In the

----

[13]Marcus Hanna Boulware, *The Oratory of Negro Leaders 1900-1968* (Westport
CT: Negro University Press, 1969) 183.

light of this, is it not incredible that any would dare preach? Is it not even more incredible to address tough, complex, controversial, critical issues with the blatant insubordination and complicity involved? But preaching is a presumptuous business at best. It is an incredible undertaking, anyway. Omitting social reality from preaching does not make the task more credible. Those who preach may as well adhere to the divine mandate and proclaim the controversial, social crisis conscious word "in season and out."

The accomplishments of this incredible undertaking have been—and continue to be—impressive. The prophetic preaching of Richard Allen brought into being a great church that combined the Jewish and Christian heritage with the African heritage and repudiated the preachments of the bishops of bigotry. When Washington Gladden and Walter Rauschenbusch preached, they caused the dawning of a new social consciousness and a renewed look at the Christian gospel. The eloquent, moving, profound and uncompromising proclamations of Mordecai Wyatt Johnson were as responsible as anything else for the development of Howard University into one of the greatest institutions of higher education in the land. The conservative religious establishment was shaken by the powerful and impassioned preaching of Harry Emerson Fosdick. The preaching of Howard Thurman, complete with its opaque and translucent windows, as he once described an aspect of preaching, brought forth a heightened sense of spirituality and demonstrated the compatibility of mysticism and social action. When Martin Luther King stood up to preach, 50,000 descendants of African slaves marched in the Cradle of the Confederacy and millions became involved in a new social revolution.

Preaching is no mere human undertaking. Those who set upon this work from the highest motivations are those who understand the depth of meaning of the spiritual that says, "I know the Lord has laid his hands on me!" Preaching is no trivial matter circumscribed by human foibles and abridged agenda. It is a divine-human enterprise and is properly concerned with the whole of life. Concern with social crises is not simply permissible in preaching: it is *imperative*. This is no elective course, no peripheral concern of the Christian gospel. It is its major thrust. Without it preaching is weak and anemic and is hardly worth the name. Authentic preaching takes into account the social issues and dilemmas that plague the human family. It is sensitive to the relevancy of the Christian gospel for these concerns and it proclaims that relevancy.

The interest here is in social crisis preaching. This is not a concern with social crisis lecturing nor with the presentation of social crisis addresses or orations, though these are important. The concern is with the proclamation of that which is crucially relevant within the context of the Christian gospel in times that are critical in terms of social dynamics and machinations. Foundational to this concern with social crisis preaching, however, is a consideration of the meaning and function of preaching itself. While a detailed treatment of the meaning of preaching must be reserved for later, some things must be said at the present time.

Richard Lischer defines preaching as "the event in which one person (or more) addresses others with the gospel."[14] In short, preaching is simply the proclamation of the Christian gospel. It is a preacher presenting the good news about Jesus Christ to others. Howard Thurman transcends the Christological element when he describes the sermon as the revelation of the working of the spirit of God upon the mind and spirit of the preacher. By this he does not mean to evade social responsibility. The sermon for Thurman is not a purely vertical affair in terms of its scope. The working of the spirit upon the human individual always has reference to one's relationship to fellow members of the human family. It is incomplete when it stops with the divine relationship and does not express itself in terms of human relationships. Preaching aims at reaching the innermost recesses of the human spirit even while expressing social concerns. It must embody the ancient past without exhibiting the burden of temporal distance.

MAKING THE WORD PRESENT

Preaching is the divine-human event in which words are used to proclaim the Word of God. It is not only the proclamation of what God has said; it is proclamation of *what God continues to say* to the pres-

---

[14]Richard Lischer, *A Theology of Preaching* (Nashville TN: Abingdon, 1981) 12.

ent condition. It is God's communication with the human family through human instrumentality. It is the spirit of God working upon the mind and spirit of the preacher with the directions that he or she proclaim the powerful, critically relevant, uncompromising Word of the living God.

Jean-Jacques von Allmen makes the significant point that preaching has the function of making the Word of God present to generations other than those of the first Christian century. Through preaching the central event of human history is made contemporary and the whole world is caused to assemble around that event. The event is that "the Word became flesh and dwelt among us, full of grace and truth" (John 1:14). The proper proclamation of that event challenges the brokenness of the human family and aims at effecting a society governed by love and justice. That Word is not locked in a prison of the ancient past. It is made contemporary through preaching. That event cannot be understood apart from its reflection of critical social issues and its meaning for social victims.[15]

Let us be reminded that the Word of God is God's communication with the human family. It is God speaking to women and men. This means what some have called the canonical witness of scripture, but it goes beyond that. It is God addressing the human condition as it is at present. Preaching has a unifying function because it assembles the world around the incarnational event and addresses the world's issues through that event.

In order for preaching to fulfill its unifying function and to carry on its responsibility to make the Word present in generations other than those historically associated with the event, it has certain gaps to bridge on its own acknowledged terrain. To put it another way, quality preaching involves the demonstration of certain vital relationships. This is an essential function of effective preaching, but it is not always easily accomplished.

Through preaching, the Word of God *demonstrates the relationship between ancient history and current issues*. When a passage is chosen from an ancient document called the Bible for the purpose of providing a

---

[15]See James H. Cone's, *A Black Theology of Liberation*, 197-227; and Howard Thurman's *Jesus and the Disinherited* (Nashville: Abingdon, 1949) in its entirety.

basis for preaching to contemporary persons about contemporary concerns, the need for the demonstration of this relationship is evident. No sermon is properly a mere recital of historical data with no direct reference to current issues. As Dwight Stevenson puts it, the sermon must not be an echo in a museum. The function of history in preaching is not fulfilled with the mere use of episodes and events as examples or models, although this obviously has its place. Rather, it is an understanding that certain events and insights of the distant past are made current by the Word of God. The Word of God that emerges during a particular era is not locked in that time frame. The Word transcends the boundaries of time even though a particular event in history may provide the occasion for its emergence. The Word is inseparable from the events that provide the setting for its communication, yet, it transcends them. The Word of God, as it evinces its presence in history, must be understood as addressing issues and concerns in this day. It must impact itself upon the contemporary scene. The concern here is not with the lessons of history, although there is much to be said for what can be learned from it; rather, the concern is with how the past can become contemporary. There is a difference. It is clear that the present becomes the past (today becomes yesterday tomorrow). The emphasis here is that, by virtue of the Word of God, the *past becomes the present*.

It must be understood that there is a difference between the manifestation of the Word in history and historical events themselves. The former transcends the latter.

The gap between ancient history and current issues seems more easily spanned when the primary category of concern is the oppressed. The record of the Word of God contained in scripture speaks more clearly to circumstances of social stress and crisis than to any other circumstance. That Word takes on special meaning when preachers assume their social responsibility as servants of the Word. The timelessness of the Word is manifested in a special manner when it is seen in terms of its relevance for social dilemmas.

The Bible—a record of the Word of God—has a special interest in the oppressed and, consequently, holds great interest for them. Generally, it may be said that the Old Testament is the record of the pursuit of a special agreement regarding the relationship between God and an oppressed people (cf. Leviticus 26:12). The New Testament is centered around one who began his ministry resolved to "set at liberty the oppressed" (Luke 4:18). There is no wonder, then, that a special hermeneutical capacity comes with oppression.

The ability of the slave preachers to ferret the real meaning out of the distorted gospel hurled to the slave balconies is phenomenal. These were not persons of exegetical sophistication—nor hermeneutical expertise. Yet, they found in the Word of God the fermentation for insurrection and a basis for hope. This is precisely because there is a bias in the direction of the oppressed and the powerless in the record of the Word. Some of the sermons included in Justo González's volume, *Proclaiming the Acceptable Year*, give graphic demonstration of this fact. For example, Choan-Seng Song's sermon, "Truth-Power and Love-Power in a Court of Law," brings alive the otherwise difficult Luke 21:12-15.[16] Another example is Gayraud S. Wilmore who sees Ezekiel 12:2-3,6 as a basis for a sermon on "Blackness as Sign and Assignment" by substituting the color of blackness for the baggage that Ezekiel carried.[17]

Von Allmen characterizes the preaching task as one of translating. That which is "present" in the Word is there; it simply must be translated by the preacher. Obviously, the translation spoken of here involves more than mere recourse to dictionaries and lexicons. One must understand that this is not the kind of translation in which so much is lost in the process that the meaning is unclear and misleading. Rather, quality preaching is like the Pentecost experience when "each one heard them speaking in his own language" (Acts 2:6b RSV). This occurs partly because of the commitment and capacity of the preacher and partly because of the power of the Word itself. Neither is dispensable.

J. Randall Nichols uses the metaphor of the freeze-drying process to illustrate how a text can be made present:

> . . . the metaphor of the modern freeze-drying food process suggests how a text might function as a repository of potential experience and significance,

---

[16]Appendix A, below.

[17]Appendix B, below.

which awaits the additive of a hearer-reader's contemporary participation to be reconstituted *in all its original meaning and fullness.*[18]

While Nichols places this observation under the caption, "An Eisegesis Revival," the contention can be made that this is not eisegesis in that, as he says, "the emergent meaning of the text loses nothing of its originality, its claim, or its otherness as it happens in contemporary hermeneutical experience."

This is the miracle that must be performed by the preaching task. Making the Word present involves recognizing the differences of the past, present, and future as well as their linear connections, but the case does not rest there. Through quality preaching the Word *becomes* what is needed in that situation while remaining the same in substance. That is the nature and the power of the Word of God.

The ancient history that serves as an instrumentality for the conveyance of the Word becomes present by serving as a mirror for the believing community. James A. Sanders's insight is helpful:

> It is the nature of the canon to be contemporized; it is . . . a mirror for the identity of the believing community, which in any era turns to ask who it is and what it is to do, even today . . . [The believing] community sees its current tensions, between what it is and what it ought to be, in the tension which Israel and the early church also experienced.[19]

It is a function of preaching to cause the past to become present in this manner. When preaching exhibits a chasm between ancient history and current concerns, it fails in terms of its potential and promise. Proclamation of the Word through scripture spans the chasm between ancient history and contemporary concerns. It is well, as someone has interpreted Barth as suggesting, to have the Bible in one hand and the newspaper in the other, but it is also important to realize that the Word *itself* is as current as the morning newspaper.

----

[18]J. Randall Nichols, *Building the Word* (San Francisco: Harper & Row Publishers, 1980) 27.

[19]James A. Sanders, *Torch and Canon* (Philadelphia: Fortress Press, 1978) xv-xvii.

There is, then, a profound relationship between the ancient history of the Bible and contemporary life and it is the responsibility and challenge of those who preach to demonstrate that relationship.

A people can be turned from futility and despair to hope, from aimless wanderings to clear direction, from the status of mere social victims to that of a people struggling productively for their own liberation through the proclamation of the Word. When that Word is proclaimed with a sense of its potential, ancient history bridges the broad chasm of the years and becomes contemporary, the eternal is expressed in time and the universal becomes concrete in space. Because of the impact of that Word, the oppressed become aware that they are not hapless orphans deserted on the doorsteps of destiny, but are sons and daughters of a caring God.

II
PERCEPTION

At heart every human being has the fidelity of the Apostle Thomas hidden in some shadowy recess, where it whispers to itself, I will not believe what I do not see and touch.

THE CONNECTICUT YANKEE
in *Steadfast* by Rose Terry

PERCEPTION AND RESPONSE

Social crisis preaching aims at eliciting a response. In traditional evangelical terms it is preaching for a decision, indeed, for a decision for Christ. True, perceptions differ as to what the words "decision for Christ" mean. The meaning here, however, is that the Christ who began his ministry with a social imperative mandated by "the spirit of the Lord" (Luke 4:18) is calling preachers to responsible social proclamation and action. When the Word is proclaimed faithfully, it is precisely that Word and that imperative. It is to understand with Paul Lehman "the radical and fulfilling difference . . . the presence of Jesus of Nazareth *in* the human story makes *to* the human story."[1] The positive response to the Word is a "decision for Christ."

Despite the authentic Word's inherent power, the desired response to it will not occur automatically. True, "we have this treasure in earthen vessels," but it is a treasure that requires intentional care in its proper use. To use another biblical metaphor, the lamp must be placed on a lampstand for maximum effectiveness. There must be access to the treasure or it is of no practical value. The light of the lamp must be visible to serve any useful purpose. Social crisis preaching, then, must take into account the issue of accessibility, which is

---

[1] As quoted in Allan Boesak, *The Finger of God* (Maryknoll NY: Orbis Books) ix.

conditioned by perception. That which is inaccurately perceived or not perceived at all is, by that measure, unavailable.

The response to social crises that comes from the Christian community will be dependent largely upon the triangular relationship between the Word, the preacher, and the congregation. The preacher has the awesome responsibility of making the crucially relevant Word accessible to the congregation. When this is done, response may be expected, for response follows perception. It must be borne in mind that response may be negative or positive although that Word, rightly presented, may be expected ultimately to elicit a positive response.

PERCEPTION AND PREACHING

Perception refers to the mental organization and interpretation of sensory data. Perception is a multifaceted phenomenon that involves the subject "sender," and the event or insight calculated to be perceived. In the present case the social crisis preacher is both subject and object. This process is conditioned by many factors, such as the properties of the stimulus itself, the emotional state of the respondent, the effects of past experiences, and attention factors such as readiness of the object to respond. Perception is a complex phenomenon but, in spite of this complexity, the proclaimer of the Christian gospel must achieve it. This is essential both for the eliciting of an action response from the hearers of the proclaimed Word and for the grasping of the Word to be proclaimed.

The nature of the response elicited by a given stimulus is conditioned by the manner in which that stimulus is perceived rather than by what it really is. If current preaching can lay claim to the high status of stimulus (though it is to be hoped, beyond the coffee variety suggested by George Bernard Shaw), the response is in some jeopardy unless appropriate attention is given to the importance of perception. Jose Miguez-Bonino refers to "pre-understanding" as a significant barrier to communication because some who comprise the congregations to which he preaches "will hear what they feel about the text, no matter what I say."[2] This is an important matter for any preaching—

---

[2] Jose Miguez-Bonino, "How Do We Hear God's Word?" in *Pastoral Hermeneutics and Ministry*, ed. Donald F. Beisswenger (prepublication edition), 1982.

and especially when that preaching is concerned with critical issues. Are those who comprise the congregation hearing what is being proclaimed or are they hearing what they feel based on "pre-understanding"? Many pastors can attest that too often members of the congregation hear what they feel regardless of what is being proclaimed. Sometimes the entire thrust of what is being presented is missed for this reason. This would be especially true regarding the presentation of highly emotional, much discussed issues. Perception is blocked or distorted by closed minds.

The perception of the congregation is vital; the perception of the proclaimer of the Word is *critical*. The proclaimer of the Word sometimes misperceives that Word and proclaims that which is tragically less than the Word of God. For example, some ministers believe the Word of God is devoid of radical social content and concern with such issues is outside the proper realm of the Christian faith. To hold to such a belief is to misperceive the Word and to deliver sermons based on this belief is to proclaim distortions and to inhibit the gospel potential. Perhaps the solemn injunction of James to prospective teachers would apply here: "Let not many of you become teachers [or preachers?] . . . for you know that we who teach [preach?] shall be judged with greater strictness" (James 3:1). A heavy responsibility, then, rests upon the proclaimer.

What the preacher understands the preaching task to be is important. What does she or he believe about the Word of God? What is social crisis preaching and what are some of the questions that must be raised regarding carrying out this responsibility effectively? In other words, what is really vital in this entire enterprise? These and other issues must be examined carefully by the proclaimer of the Word.

Perceptions of the preaching task are conditioned by many factors. These include the theological presuppositions of the denominational context. Also, its relationship to the total task of ministry is of importance. The Faith and Order Commission of the World Council of Churches provides a reminder of that which is basic in viewing the Christian ministry: "All ministry in the church is to be understood in the light of him who came, 'Not to be served, but to serve' (Mark 10:45). It is he who said 'As the Father has sent me, so I send you' (John 20:21). Thus, our calling in Christ constrains us to a

---

costly, dedicated and humble involvement in the needs of mankind."[3] This is the essence of social crisis preaching—costly, dedicated, and humble involvement in the needs of humankind. This is the difference between the town crier and the Christian preacher, P. H. Menoud explains, although the same Greek word is used for both. "A herald may be more or less indifferent to the news he proclaims. The Christian preacher, on the contrary, is a man who himself has been 'laid hold on by Christ Jesus.' "[4] It is not the mere presentation of an oration or address on a religious topic nor is it simply a report of the news—even the *good* news. It is the imperishable Word of God *through human experience*. It is involvement with that Word and it is adherence to its personal and social mandate.

THE WORD OF GOD

Social crisis preaching will more nearly achieve its potential if that task is perceived as the proclamation of the Word of God rather than something extraneous or tangential to that Word. This means the Word must be perceived as having particular relevance for circumstances of oppression and deprivation. Howard Thurman writes:

> That word, what was it?
> It was for men whose backs are against the wall;
> Whose hope feeds eternally on itself, always consuming,
>   but never consumed.[5]

It is a basic contention of liberation theologians that the Word of God is a Word of liberation. Justo and Catherine González, in referring to the Word of God as it is found in scripture, call for a "new hermeneutic" that will enable those especially concerned with the structures of oppression to experience the "joyful discovery that the Bible was

---

[3]*One Baptism, One Eucharist and A Mutually Recognized Ministry*, Faith and Order Paper No. 73 (Geneva, Switzerland: World Council of Churches, 1975).

[4]*Interpreters Dictionary of the Bible* (Nashville TN: Abingdon Press, 1962) K-Q:868.

[5]Howard Thurman, *The Mood of Christmas* (New York: Harper and Row Publishers, 1973) 112.

much more on our side than we ever dared hope."[6] This is not to join
the ranks of those who contend that the Word of God is found completely and exclusively in the Bible. Rather, it is understanding with
Iris V. and Kendig Brubaker Cully that the Bible "contains the record
of God's Word."[7]

The great disparity in the perception of the Word of God in-
creases the incidence of highly explosive emotional land mines in the
area to be traversed. The current era of aggressive religious conservatism insures that this disparity will abide for yet a long time. Those
on the religious right tend to be intolerant of and to regard as "enemies" those whose perspectives are different. It is especially important to bear in mind that religious conservatism is often, though not
always, associated with political and social conservatism. The implications of this for social crisis preaching are obvious.

Basically, it may be said that the Word of God is God's living communication with members of the human family. It is dynamic in quality and imperative in mood. It is auditory and visual although
primacy is given to auditory perception. From the days of the Old
Testament to the present the Word has been received through hearing. The Bible records instances when visions were received, but
many of these were accompanied with the auditory.

In the Old Testament the term "Word of God" refers to (1) God's
actual utterances, which prophets and seers heard directly from God
and could pass along; (2) messages from God which may come in the
form of visions or symbolic acts that require interpretation; (3) words
spoken by prophets that are understood to be equivalent to what the
prophet heard from God; and (4) written messages that can become
a part of the heritage of the community. The term "Word" in the New
Testament is closely related to that of the Old Testament, but there
are added dimensions. For example, in the New Testament the Word
becomes flesh (John 1:14). Also, in the New Testament the term
means the Old Testament law (Mark 7:13); other Old Testament

---

[6]Justo González and Catherine González, *Liberation Preaching* (Nashville TN:
Abingdon Press, 1980) 32.

[7]Iris V. Cully and Kendig Brubaker Cully, *An Introductory Theological Word Book*
(Philadelphia: The Westminster Press, 1943) 202.

passages (e.g., John 10:35); the preaching of Jesus (Luke 5:1); and the revealed will of God (Romans 9:6 et al.).

Bernard W. Anderson calls the Word of God "Metaphorical language to refer to God's establishing a personal, I-thou relationship with his people."[8] Thus, the Word of God is the initiative of God in divine to human communication that accords dignity to members of the human family. It is the Word of Good News for the disinherited and the dispossessed.

The Word of canonical scripture is not synonymous with the Word of God. As suggested earlier, the scriptural Word is *a* (not *the*) record that *human beings* write "Of the Word of God as channeled through the history and experiences that they preserved."

It must be clear that the proclaimer of the crisis-conscious gospel not only bases his or her message upon the Word of God as found in scripture, but the very sermon proclaimed is, ideally, the Word of God. It is the event of God still speaking to humanity. It is the Word of God made present. The very scripture itself comes alive in proclamation. Ancient history becomes current. The past becomes present. This is the miracle of preaching.

In the scriptures several characteristics of the Word of God are presented. It will not return empty (Isaiah 55:11); it "will stand forever" (Isaiah 40:8); it takes on specificity and it incorporates; it transcends the personality of the proclaimer; it is dynamic and piercing (Hebrews 4:12); and it is accompanied by manifestations of divine power (Hebrews 2:4), and so forth.

When the social crisis-conscious preacher mounts the rostrum she or he has the responsibility of proclaiming the Word of God in all of its uncompromising power. It is a Word that speaks to the condition of the oppressed. It informs, it energizes, it convicts, it converts, and it blazes the trail for social changes. The Word of God is not static and placid; it is dynamic and unrelentingly disturbing. Jeremiah's metaphor is apt—it is a fire! Who can ignore a raging fire? Something of the dynamism of the Word of God on behalf of the oppressed is implicit in these words of James H. Cone: "God's Word in Christ not

---

[8]Bernard W. Anderson, *The Living Word of the Bible* (Philadelphia: The Westminster Press, 1979) 16.

only fulfills his purpose for man through his elected people, but also inaugurates a new age in which all oppressed people become his people."[9]

THE MEANING OF
SOCIAL CRISIS PREACHING

Social crisis preaching is the proclamation of that which is crucially relevant within the context of the Christian gospel in times of social upheaval and stress. It aims at setting corrective measures into motion. Social crisis preaching is calculated to yield a practical good with regard to the most painful problems of society. It is deeply rooted in the history and meaning of the Christian faith.

Crisis is a transliteration of the Greek word κρίσις, which means in that context judgment, parting, estrangement, separation. Interestingly enough, Frederich Büchsel states that in the Septuagint, the term κρίσις means "a sense of the right, especially the right of the oppressed which is vindicated by the judge."[10] There he cites Matthew 23:20 and Luke 11:42 pointing out that the reproach against the Pharisees was due to their indifference to the poor. While this does not exhaust the meaning of the term in its original language, it is particularly important for our purposes here as it reveals that in its most primitive use, the term "crisis" had social content and meaning.

The term in its current usage refers to a decisive moment, to a turning point or "an unstable or crucial time or state of affairs."[11] It often has reference to physical illness. Van Nostrand's *Scientific Encyclopedia* is graphic in defining the term: "the turning point in a disease, either toward recovery or death." For sickle-cell anemia sufferers the term does not refer as much to the crossroad between recovery and death as it does to intense pain. This is especially true of the most painful crisis, called basoclusive crisis, which occurs when

---

[9]James H. Cone, *Black Theology and Black Power* (New York: Seabury Press, 1969) 69.

[10]G. Kittel, trans. G. W. Bromiley, *Theological Dictionary of the New Testament* (Grand Rapids MI: Wm. B. Eerdmans Publishing Company, 1965) 3:942.

[11]*Webster's Seventh New Collegiate Dictionary* (Springfield MA: G. and C. Merriam Company, Publishers, 1967).

the sickle cells clog up the small capillaries of the circulatory system so that the normal cells carrying oxygen cannot get through.

There is a sense in which the use of the term in its present case gathers up most of these meanings. It not only has social content, the poor and the oppressed comprise a major category of concern, as is the emphasis in the Septuagint rendering. Periods of social crisis involve decisive moments and turning points. Sometimes the social crisis that must be addressed through preaching is as serious as the physical crisis described by Van Nostrand: it is a turning point either toward recovery or death. How vital it is for the preacher to be aware of this volatility. Add to this the explosiveness of the Word of God and it becomes clearer that the preachers' responsibility is no inconsiderable matter. Also, it demonstrates the incendiary quality of the tongue: "How great a forest is set ablaze by a small fire! And the tongue is a fire . . ." (James 3:5b, 6a).

The present concern is with social crises, such as those circumstances, situations, principles, decisions, and actions that impact upon people collectively and usually negatively. Crises result from political arrangements, governmental action or inaction, the functioning of particular groups or individuals within society, and other conditions or actions. Wars, civil uprising, economic depression, epidemics, responses to injustice such as rebellions, and the like are examples of social crises. Crises may be personal or social, although those that are considered to be personal are also social, for these two cannot be ultimately separated.

In spite of the explosive nature of the circumstances against which social crisis preaching must take place, the preacher aims at eliciting an action response and this presupposes perception of the topic at least by the preacher.

Sometimes it is useful to ask pertinent questions regarding an issue and the people to whom it is to be presented in sermon form. Even as this is done it is well to accept the limitations of the questioning process. Questions call for answers but problems require solutions. Abraham Heschel is clear at this point:

> To ask a question is an act of the intellect; to face a problem is a situation involving the whole person. A question is the result of thirst for knowledge; a

problem reflects a state of perplexity or even distress. A question calls for an answer, a problem calls for a solution.[12]

This process of questioning, however, can serve as a step in the direction of problem solving, which is what social crisis preaching is all about. Heschel does acknowledge that a certain level of questioning "is more than to seek an approach to an answer; it is a breakthrough."[13] Some questions related to perception and social crisis preaching must be raised. These are questions that have to do with the triangular relationship between the Word of God, the preacher, and the congregation, particularly as they address critical social issues. These questions may not be audibly raised; rather, they may well be part of the meditation that the minister does in preparation for the proclamation of the gospel. Some such questions as these must comprise part of that preparation: "*What* social crisis?" "Who are these people?" "Why are they here?" "What do I perceive their needs to be?" and "What can I do about it?"

QUESTIONS RELATED TO PERCEPTION AND SOCIAL CRISIS PREACHING

What Social Crisis? The enthusiastic and skillful proclamation of a committed preacher will be of no avail if the hearers perceive there to be no crisis. The preacher is ill-equipped to deal sermonically with critical social issues unless he or she comes to grips with this question. Sometimes the question, What social crisis? comprises the unformed words of many in the congregation. Then, there are times when it is an unsettled question in the heart of hearts of the minister. It is an urgent consideration.

Sometimes the preacher who does not really perceive that there is a serious crisis will simply decry the evil of the times in the attempt to salve his or her conscience and to satisfy certain elements in the congregation. This kind of approach may be of some small value, but will not suffice in a world that is aflame with specific issues and prob-

---

[12]Abraham Heschel, *Who Is Man?* (Stanford CA: Stanford University Press, 1965) 1.

[13]Ibid., 5.

lems. The preacher cannot handle critical social issues with broad generalities. There must be full awareness of the existence and nature of crises in order for them to be effectively addressed.

While the mantle of the prophets rests upon the shoulders of the preacher and by that token these responsibilities are in some way special, that preacher is part and parcel of the fabric of this society and will share some of the frustrations and confusions that he or she must address. Lack of clarity or of conviction regarding a given social crisis may be expected.

Although much of the social evil that exists is willful, social ignorance is a major problem for pulpit and pew alike. It is sometimes alarming to discover how woefully uninformed persons in responsible positions are when it comes to matters of injustice and general racism. Those who exhibit great knowledge of other matters, such as how to develop a successful business, often reveal the absence of elementary understanding of matters that pertain to some aspects of social reality. They are often abysmally ignorant of the problems that have victimized so many in this country for so long and they are even less aware of their own complicity.

Social ignorance is made all the more pervasive and devastating by a society that has so butchered recorded history as to present a patently false picture of the past. Its chroniclers have shoved aside corpora of experience that clash with the picture of this society being presented or that would depict a people within that society in a more positive light than would serve the cause of racism. Thus, Blacks in the United States have had to rummage through closets of their own past and come up with a polemical contention regarding their place in American history. The title of a book authored by the late Merle R. Epps in the thirties demonstrates this polemical spirit: *The Negro, too, In American History.*

This has meant that many White Americans are uninformed and misinformed about this amazing and critically important body of experience. This lack of information expresses itself in views all the way from blatant racism—belief in the congenital inferiority of a people—to the glib contention that the status of Blacks is no different from that of others who are deprived in this society. This lack of information is equally as serious when Blacks themselves are misinformed about their own experiences.

Perhaps it would be well for any preacher to raise the question occasionally, "What social crisis?" if this inquiry will cause the preacher to examine the issues along with himself or herself in pursuit of the response. The dispelling of social ignorance is vital in the proclamation of the crisis conscious Word.

There are social crises confronting every preacher in the United States constantly and it is incumbent upon him or her to discern adequately the nature of that crisis and to assume his or her responsibility regarding it.

Practical suggestions may be in order for those who are in pursuit of an answer to this question.

(1) *Recognize the preacher's limitations in the inquiry*. Any who have worked in the civil rights movement or other social causes will be familiar with the handicap caused by persons whose hearts are nearly in the right place but who over-identify with social victims. One thinks of the time when there were Black rebellions in many parts of the United States and the understanding was that any place that was not identifiably Black stood in danger of being destroyed during the uprisings. One cartoonist drew the picture of a perplexed President Lyndon Johnson nervously peering out of the White House window. There was a sign on the gate of the White House that read "soul brother." It is unhelpful to the cause to pretend these limitations do not exist and to bury one's head in the sand. The better part of wisdom is to face these limitations honestly and to deal with them creatively.

The limitations that the preacher has may have many causes. Among these are *experience*, *theological orientation*, and the pressure of *practical considerations*.

Although there are times when individuals seem to transcend particular experiences of their lives and identify understandably with positions and causes that run counter to their experiences, the factor of experience is still persuasive and compelling. If the crisis has to do with the international situation, it may easily be understood that preachers and others would be limited in their understanding of the intricacies of the issues. Also in the matter of race, those who are outside the cultural experiences of those being oppressed must acknowledge that this absence of experiential orientation is a delimiting factor.

There are many who now contend that theological orientation lies somewhere near the root of the race problem in America. The late theologian Jean Russell in *God's Lost Cause* sees historical theology as a major cause of the racial problems in America. Liberation theologians and particularly theologians of the Black experience see theological posture as critically relevant in terms of social crises that center upon the oppressed. One's theology reflects itself in attitudes towards war in general and the nuclear bomb in particular. A recent Gallup poll revealed that those who are most concerned about the poor and whose actions reveal this concern are persons of religious commitment which, of course, stems from some theological understanding.

Practical considerations may also blind the minister to certain manifestations of social reality. For example, the pastor's commitment to keeping ecclesiastical machinery oiled may preclude his or her giving necessary attention to social issues and concerns. Building programs, fund raising, and the like, often loom large in the schedule and energy budget of the minister and this may limit his or her understanding of issues. The preacher's own material comfort and personal economy must not be overlooked as possible reasons for his or her limitations.

(2) *Tap available human resources*. In most communities there are persons who can be of help to members of the clergy and others who are interested in understanding the nature and character of existing crises and their implications for ministry. Educational institutions, news media organizations, community organizations are among the places to look for human resources to aid in this endeavor. Often there are persons among the members of the congregations who have more than average knowledge regarding given crises.

Obviously, care must be taken to avoid involving counterproductive human resources. There are always persons who are so passionate in the pursuit of a certain course that great reliability cannot be placed in their factual accuracy. It is important, however, for human resources who represent different points of view to be invited to assist. Those whose positions are unorthodox may be among the most useful resources. This may not bear out John Haynes Holmes's comment that light sometimes comes through a crack! Rather, it is to understand that the best information does not always come from the easygoing, noncontroversial persons who are sometimes called into the picture to help address critical issues. Those who are generally categorized as radicals are often, though not always, well informed and can articulate their positions on issues. It is not likely that the gentle, "all-things-to-all-people" person will be able to represent adequately the frustration, embitterment, anger, hopes, and dreams of a downtrodden people.

During a time of severe racial crisis in a certain city, the city officials were quite surprised to learn that Black college administrators selected by them were unacceptable to the Black masses as their spokespersons. These persons were well respected as *educators* in that community. It was simply clear that they could not articulate the mood and perceived need of the Black community generally.

(3) *Utilize published materials that address current social issues.* Much has been written that deals, in one way or another, with existing crises. Some of these materials will be very helpful while others may be of questionable value. These are in the form of books, periodicals, denominational and interdenominational documents. Works in the general area of liberation theology and liberation ethics are certain to be of value. Periodicals such as the *Christian Century, Christianity and Crisis, Sojourners, The Black Scholar, The Other Side, Social Action,* and *Engage/Social Action* will be useful for the minister who desires further enlightenment on social crises. Again, it is helpful to secure works representing opposing points of view and to study all sides of the issue. All of the writings of Martin Luther King, Jr. are amazingly relevant and useful older works such as the writings of Walter Rauschenbusch and Ernst Troeltsch are of abiding value in the quest. Black newspapers and literature represent an important literary resource.

(4) *Become directly involved in the issues.* Sometimes the preacher will be tempted to present the experiences of others as illustrative matter while addressing critical social issues rhetorically, but never really to identify herself/himself with the issues of the community. If he or she is almost totally uninformed, the gospel places him or her under a moral and religious obligation to become informed as the first step in becoming involved. Some of the issues are quite clear in terms of the Christian imperative. One can easily identify with the morally tena-

ble side of the issue while seeking to learn more of its detailed meaning.

The sermon must never become the *social cosmos* of the preacher. Sometimes the words and actions of the preacher are in two entirely different columns. What one does or leaves undone often speaks much more persuasively than words—whether sermonic or otherwise.

The preacher must find answers to the question "What social crisis?" and ignorance of the fact is no justifiable excuse. She or he must take advantage of all opportunities to learn what the contemporary scene is like as she or he is divinely appointed to do something about it.

M. Kent Millard in an article entitled "Thinking about Social Issues" in the December 1982 issue of *Engage/Social Action*, presented an educational model to help Christians relate their understanding of the faith to social issues. The three components are (1) a factual phase, during which the gathering and presentation of basic facts will take place; (2) the biblical and theological phase, when biblical experiences, inferences, and injunctions will be studied; and (3) the personal decision phase during which the members of the congregation will be helpful with the process of making their own decisions regarding the issues at hand. This procedure may be helpful in the identification and the addressing of critical social issues.

Who Are These People? While it may sometimes appear to be a fruitless quest, every preacher knows the importance of having the means of learning something of the congregation to which she or he is to preach. One may not be able to learn as much as is desired, but it is important to know as much as possible about those who are expected to perceive the message correctly and to act upon it. This is especially important for social crisis preaching. The concern here is mainly with preachers who are pastors of the congregations to whom the social crisis preaching is delivered. Pastors should, by virtue of their pastoral function and relation, be aware of some of the needs and desires of the congregation.

Who the people are is urgent for a consideration of what is to be said to them and how it is to be said. Who are these people? They are broadly diverse. They are men and women, the young and the old, who are caught in the web of life. They are dreamers and they are those who have forgotten how to dream. They are well educated, they are poorly educated. They are economically solvent, they are hard-pressed economically. They are socially ignorant and they are latent social activists.

Those who comprise the congregations of preachers have their own crises that must not be disregarded. Frustrations and unfulfilled hopes characterize them. They have been recipients of misguided assertions regarding people different from themselves and they are persons with an openness to all people, no matter how different they may appear to be.

Who are they? They are people who are not excited about the social issue that the preacher is going to present in sermon context. They are people with their own priorities—quite different from those of the preacher. They may be insensitive to injustice and other glaring wrongs. They may be fatalistic and feel it is useless to pursue the issues about which the minister is passionately concerned. They may be receptive, concerned, and informed.

Once the preacher becomes enlightened as to who the people are before whom the social crisis sermons must be delivered, he or she will have an informed perspective on how crisis sermon delivery can best be done.

Through workshops, seminars, counseling, sermons, institutes, denominational literature, and other resources the pastor prepares her or his people for impending crises.

Why Are They Here? The preacher will be wise to recognize that all who come to the place of worship do not necessarily come for the highest purposes. Some have come because it is their habit to be at that place at that time. Some come because it is good for business or the profession or the reputation. This is not to suggest that all who assemble at a worship setting gather there for the wrong reasons. To be sure, many come "as an empty pitcher before a full fountain," as a Black folk expression has it. They come because it is the most appropriate place to be at that time and they come with eager anticipation. They come with a sense of expectancy.

Sermon preparation and delivery must take into account the variety of reasons the congregation gathers. The extent to which the preacher can communicate effectively may be determined by why they are there in the first place. If they have come for trivial reasons, their level of expectation is not likely to be very high and their receptivity will be conditioned by this fact. If they come to have their prejudices confirmed, the preacher with a message of social crisis import on the morally tenable side of the issue is likely to confront serious barriers to communication. On the other hand, if the congregation is aware that something has occurred or is occurring in the community or nation or world and they know their minister is sensitive to these matters and provides leadership as necessary, communication will be greatly facilitated.

The preacher has the responsibility to be as aware as possible of whom the people are who comprise his or her congregation. As Edgar N. Jackson put it, "The capacity for sensitivity, the ability to feel with and for his [or her] people, is the pastor's supreme art." The pastor must see the congregation "not as a multitude . . . [but must be] sensitive to the multitude as a group of individual souls."[14] While it is not practical to expect to know all of the members of most congregations personally and intimately, the pastor can be sensitive to this need. This will mean providing experiences that will increase awareness of the members' stands on issues such as justice, peace, and so forth. The pastor would do well to look at the files of members occasionally to ascertain such information as vocations, their academic training, their family backgrounds, their work in the church, their special interests, and so forth. Churches may choose to have members write a brief statement of faith for their files. While all will not consider this to be a desirable and appropriate inquiry, others find it useful in their performance of ministry.

As Edwin McNeil Poteat suggests, how one deals with another is determined in large measure by what and who he or she understands the other to be.[15]

What Are Their Needs? Preaching is no mere rhetorical exercise. It is not even the presentation of Bible lesson. It is the act of addressing human need with divine and human resources. In order to accom-

---

[14]Edgar N. Jackson, *A Psychology for Preaching* (Great Neck NY: Channel Press, Inc., 1969) 64.

[15]Edwin McNeil Poteat, *God Makes the Difference* (New York: Harper & Brothers, 1951) 50ff.

plish this, the preacher must be sensitive to both the need and the resources. Beyond this, of course, must be the skill to get the two together creatively. Perceptions of need vary widely. Not only is there likely to be a great divergence in the perception of need between preacher and people; such a divergence exists among people themselves and sometimes individuals are inconsistent as to what they understand their own needs to be.

Kahlil Gibran's petition in the treatise on Prayer in *The Prophet* summarizes it theologically: "Thou art our need; and in giving us more of thyself thou giveth us all." It is essential, however, to give attention to the specific needs of the people. This includes their obvious needs as well as the needs that they do not realize they have. It includes personal needs as well as those that are social.

It must be understood that the people's perception of their needs is not irrelevant, although that perception may be based upon a false reading of reality and may in fact, be quite the opposite of their actual needs. The minister must seek to know what they understand their needs to be while at the same time trying to understand what the minister himself/herself perceives these needs to be.

The Christian imperative notwithstanding, persons will see social crises as reflecting their own needs only when these crises are related to their circumstances in an obvious way. The problems of those who live in the central city are not likely to be seen by suburbanites as of any practical concern to them until those problems begin to reveal that they cannot, in fact, be confined to the central city. For the minister to decry apartheid in South Africa may seem totally irrelevant to persons in this country until it is shown how apartheid is fed by conscious and unconscious economic transactions in and by the United States. It is often necessary, then, for the preacher to demonstrate some interpretation of the needs that she or he will be addressing and their relationship to the concerns of those who comprise the congregation.

Although precise answers are not likely to be possible, it is important for the social crisis preacher to ask the question, "What are their needs?" and then to pursue the answer as fully as possible. Otherwise, the minister may be answering questions no one is asking and engaging in the proverbial scratching them where they do not itch.

What Can I Do About It? After taking care in the endeavor to find answers to certain vital questions and thus to correct errors or distortions of perception, the preacher must be concerned with what he or she can do about all of this. These inquiries are no mere academic exercises to increase the preacher's knowledge about people and conditions. Rather, the ultimate purpose is to enable him or her to pursue the work of ministry more faithfully and more efficiently.

When the minister raises the question, "What can I do about it?" this is no trivial matter. What qualifies the preacher to do anything about it? He or she is caught in the same circumstances and is part of the same society. The minister has prejudices, narrowness, sick perspectives just as do others. Yet, the responsibility is clear: God has ordained that the gospel be proclaimed by vulnerable human beings. No angels have been sent to do this chore. For better or for worse, in sickness or in health, it is human responsibility.

Allan Boesak speaks a word for all whose responsibility is to proclaim the Word when he says of the Black preachers in South Africa that they must speak the Word of God. "A Word that shows a way out of the darkness of oppression, poverty, and misery. A word that is an inspiration to active participation in God's struggle for justice and liberation, yet at the same time is not itself an expression of demagogy. A word that holds on to the truth that God is on the side of the oppressed and that he, if they put their trust in him, will deliver them from the power of the oppressor—as he did in the past."[16] What can the preacher do? Why, speak the powerful, uncompromising Word—that is the most relevant thing he or she can do. Rudolph Bohren is right: "The greatest deed [one] can do... is to proclaim the word."[17] That word is as current as the social crises that confront this beleaguered generation and it is more powerful than any of the forces that beset and intimidate. It is the *living* Word of the *living* God. In the record of the Word it is written:

For as the rain and the snow come down from heaven,

---

[16]Allan Boesak, *The Finger of God*, 2.

[17]Rudolph Bohren, *Preaching and Community* (Richmond VA: John Knox Press, 1965) 17.

and return not thither and water the earth,
making it bring forth and sprout,
giving seed to the sower and bread to the eater,
so shall my word be that goes forth from my mouth;
it shall not return to me empty,
but it shall accomplish that which I purpose,
and prosper in the thing for which I sent it.

—Isaiah 55:10,11.

The power inherent in that word conjoined with the perceptiveness, commitment, and faithfulness of the preacher who proclaims that word and the people who hear it, will bring results.

III
PERSPECTIVE

In all of the difficulties which arise in life, fling yourself down on the truth and cling to that as a drowning man in a stormy sea flings himself onto a plank and clings to it, knowing that, whether he sink or swim with it, it is the best he has. If you become a man of thought and learning, oh, never with your left hand be afraid to pull down what your right hand has painfully built up through the years of thought and study, if you see it at last not to be founded on that which is; die poor, un-loved, unknown, a failure—but shut your eyes to nothing that seems to them the reality.[1]

---

[1]Howard Thurman, ed., *A Track to the Water's Edge, The Olive Schreiner Reader* (New York: Harper and Row Publishers, 1973) 153.

INTRODUCTORY STATEMENT

In *Embezzled Heaven* Franz Werfel makes the point that a picture without perspective is flatness itself, and that without perspective everything is meaningless. The word "perspective" is derived from two Latin words which, combined, mean "to look through." It is a way of picturing or viewing objects or entities as they actually are including all their dimensions, relationships, and distances. In short, it is an attempt to look at things thoroughly. It transcends flatness and meaninglessness. Thus, since social crisis preaching does not appear in isolation from other realities, our present task is to view it from the perspective of history, the Bible, and the Black experience.

In spite of Carl Sandburg's quip that history is a bucket of ashes and Samuel Butler's charge that while God cannot alter the past, historians can, historical perspective is important in considering social crisis preaching. Like prophetism, social crisis preaching is based on an understanding of history that accepts meaning in terms of divine involvement. This perspective is urgent not only because its lessons inform and warn, but also because there is a certain currency about history. It aids in the proclamation of the Word of God, which thereby becomes present in generations other than those depicted in the historical era out of which it emerges. To view social crisis preaching from a historical perspective is to search for and lay hold on those experiences through which the Word of God is mediated.

Biblical perspective is vital and irreplaceable for social crisis preaching. It is important for this perspective to be explored, especially in view of the fact that the Bible has often been used as an instrument of oppression rather than as an instrument for human liberation. In all candor, it lends itself to both uses. One's perspective may determine which use will be employed. In the Bible, human existence is linked to eternal destiny. Humanity is seen against the background of divinity. What members of the human family perpetrate or are victimized by has divine significance. The Bible—the record of the Word of God—is a major source for social crisis preaching. At all points it must be borne in mind that God is not mute outside the Bible; it is conceivable that his speech may even be heard in some of the dogma of the church.

The corpus of experience most overlooked in the pursuit of virtually any study is the Black experience. Only within very recent years have a few of those who write and lecture in certain disciplines begun to pay token attention to the Black presence in America and the world; and that only while the "natives are restless." The prevailing point of view, one fears, is that non-white pigmentation is synonymous with inferiority. The Black experience, however, is a reality with which this society must reckon. Vincent Harding presents it forcefully:

> Just as America can know no survival worth considering unless it finds a way of facing its black counter image, so too, our history is a tale told by fools if it does not incorporate the Afro-American past with unflinching integrity.[2]

Black existence in America has been one of continuous social crisis. Virtually all of the preaching that Blacks do is social crisis preaching, although some preaching is cleverly disguised. The Black religious experience must be of paramount importance in the discussion of any human experience, most especially in the field of religion.

It should be clear that these perspectives are not mutually exclusive. One cannot, for example, discuss historical perspective without

[2]Martin Marty, ed., *New Theology No. 6* (Nashville TN: Abingdon Press) 168.

beginning with the Bible and including some attention to the Black experience. Similarly, the biblical perspective will involve the historical. The place of preaching within the total context of ministry is informed by historical and biblical experiences and is reflected in the Black experience.

HISTORICAL PERSPECTIVE

Paul Tillich's observation that "the historian's task is to 'make alive' what has 'passed away'"[3] underscores the importance of the historical perspective. It is not possible for the present to be detached from the past. This is true for the simple reason that the present not only emerges out of the past, but in important ways is continuous with it. That is to say, current events do not occur independent of historical antecedents.

The concern with social crisis preaching, then, cannot be expressed fully apart from the past. Some attention must be given to the question of how this issue is involved in the Jewish and Christian heritage. The present manifestations of the Jewish and Christian faiths are reflective of the involvement of critical social issues in its past. This is not to suggest historical determinism. Rather, it is to face the reality that the present cannot be severed from the past, although that past does not predetermine the specific terms of the present. Thomas Carlyle attributed all positive social change to "Great Men." Leopold von Bismarck, founder of the German Empire, said that "The Great Man can do nothing of himself, he can only lie in wait and listen until amid the march of events he can hear the footsteps of God. Then he leaps forward and grasps the hem of his garment." Usually history speaks most audibly and positively when there is an interaction between great persons and the setting or the environment. Social change agents are persons who can perceive the possibilities about themselves and who take advantage of them. This is the role and function of the social crisis preacher.

To invoke the preaching art in times of social crisis is to stand on firm historical ground. This way of addressing critical social issues is

---

[3]Paul Tillich, *Systematic Theology* (Chicago: The University of Chicago Press, 1951) 1:104.

not alien to the Christian heritage, although some would contend with vigor and passion in quite the opposite direction. It must be acknowledged that there have been persons in history who have emphasized the vertical dimension of the faith while giving scant attention to that which is horizontal. The presence of social crises did not alter these contentions, but rather tended to enlarge the presumed gap between the "spiritual" and the "social." In other words, those who decry the political and social dimension of ministry often use social crises as the occasion to proclaim their demurrer and to insist that only the vertical is vital. The authentic essence of the Christian faith demonstrates a critical social awareness and sometimes *precipitates* crises in addressing the practical concerns that grow out of that awareness. The horizontal dimension is *continuous with* the vertical. These are not separate entities.

The comment of Abraham Heschel on religion and social and political concerns is to the point. Once, when he was being interviewed, Heschel was asked to respond to those who insist that the Jewish and Christian faiths have been purely "spiritual" or "religious." His reply was that God himself does not seem to be very religious as he always gets himself involved in the social and political affairs of members of the human family.

The reality is that Christian history reveals some ambivalences towards the addressing of social issues from within the context of the faith. Historically, both "horizontalists" and "verticalists" abound. In spite of this, however, history is the setting against which the Word of God emerges. It is an arena of God's activity and a channel of God's speech. God speaks through history's high and low moments.

The Word of God has been proclaimed since the beginning of history. It has been proclaimed "in and out of season" by persons assigned by God to do so. Sometimes it has been whispered when it should have been shouted, but it has been present and audible.

DeWitte Holland suggests that, with a nontechnical use of the term "preacher," certain persons who preceded the period of prophetism may be designated by that term. (For example, Enoch, who "prophesied" according to Jude 14; Noah the "preacher of righteousness"; Abraham; and Moses, who was commissioned to take God's message to Pharaoh and tell him that God says "let my people go.") It is the prophets, however, "from whom we really date our modern Christian preaching practices."[4]

Abraham Heschel speaks of the prophets as being "one octave too high for our ears." He points out that

> We and the prophet have no language in common. To us the moral state of society, for all its stains and spots, seems fair and trim; to the prophet it is dreadful. So many deeds of charity are done, so much decency radiates day and night; yet to the prophet satiety of the conscience is prudery and flight from responsibility. Our standards are modest; our sense of injustice tolerable, timid; our moral indignation impermanent; yet human violence is interminable, unbearable, permanent. To us life is often serene, in the prophet's eye the world reels in confusion. The prophet makes no concession to man's capacity. Exhibiting little understanding for human weakness, he seems unable to extenuate the culpability of man.[5]

This observation regarding the differences that exist between the prophets and persons in contemporary society points out the need for those who wear the prophet's mantle in this day. There is current need for those who are "an octave too high." The social crisis preacher has the opportunity, like the prophet, to address issues that are being overlooked or treated lightly by the forces of religion.

The human link between the fiery proclamation of the Old Testament prophets and the preaching of Jesus was John the Baptist.[6] The biblical presentation of the work of John depicts an almost startling interlacing of political reality and the proclamation of John. Luke 3, for example, precedes the announcement that "the word of God came to John," with an identification of the political leadership. Among those who came to John for counsel and guidance were persons related to the political structure. It is amazing that tax collectors (v. 12) and soldiers (v. 14) came to John for direction rather than to their supervisors and commanding officers.

The central place of Jesus in the Christian enterprise is obvious. James Cone and Howard Thurman, approaching the matter from

---

[4]DeWitte T. Holland, *The Preaching Tradition: A Brief History* (Nashville TN: Abingdon, 1980) 13, 14.

[5]Abraham J. Heschel, *The Prophets* (New York: Harper Torchbooks, 1962) 1:9.

[6]See Holland, *The Preaching Tradition*, 16.

opposite Christological postures, both emphasize the centrality of Jesus for Christianity and for the welfare of the oppressed. "One has only to read the gospel to be convinced of the central importance of Jesus Christ in the Christian faith. According to the New Testament, Jesus is the man for others who views his existence as inextricably tied to other men to the degree that his own person is inexplicable apart from others. The others, of course, refer to all . . . , especially the oppressed, the unwanted of society, the sinner."[7] While holding to a nontraditional Christological perspective, Howard Thurman nevertheless emphasizes the centrality of Jesus, not only for Christianity, but also for the oppressed. He was fond of quoting the words of Weinel and Widgery: "They who seek God with all their hearts must, however, some day on their way meet Jesus."[8]

As will be discussed later, the Kingdom of God, which has profound social meaning, was basic in the preaching and the teaching of Jesus.

Cane Hope Felder of the Howard University Divinity School argues that the equality of persons was a major concern in the preaching of Jesus.[9] He bases this, in part, upon Mark 12:14: "Teacher we know that you are true and care for no man (i.e., the presumptuous opinion of others), for you do not regard the position of men." It must be seen that Jesus' concern for human equality means at times favoring those who are treated unfairly in order to effect equality. It is a kind of "affirmative action" disposition.

The preaching, teaching, and deeds of Jesus are central to Christian social crisis preaching. The Christian preacher who understands the importance of the inclusion of the social dimension in preaching will give primary consideration to this centrality.

The preaching of Peter is generally understood to be more or less representative of the preaching of the apostles. In the discourse to

---

[7]James H. Cone, *Black Theology and Black Power* (New York: The Seabury Press, 1969) 35.

[8]As quoted in Howard Thurman, *Jesus and the Disinherited* (Nashville TN: Abingdon Press, 1949/1969) 11.

[9]See Cane Hope Felder, "Preaching in the Ministry of Jesus," a lecture presented to the Shaw Divinity School's Seventh Annual Conference, 17-19 March 1980.

Cornelius in Acts 10:34-43, he includes the words, "Truly I perceive
that God shows no partiality," which indicates a major concern with
the issue of equality. Again, it must be stated that God, out of concern
for the issue of human equality, shows a bias concern for those who
have not been treated equally.

The preaching of Paul is seen by C. H. Dodd as representative of
apostolic preaching generally:

> Paul himself at least believed that in essentials his gospel was that of the prim-
> itive apostles; for although in Gal. 1:11-18 he states with emphasis that he did
> not derive it from any human source, nevertheless in the same epistle (2:2)
> he says that he laid "the Gospel which I preach" before Peter, James and John,
> and that they gave their approval.[10]

As is the case at the present time, however, there were likely to have
been significant differences in the preaching of the various apostles.

On the surface it would seem clear that Paul's preaching must
have had some social content inasmuch as he included a concern with
the Kingdom of God in his writing and his preaching. Acts 19:8 is but
one of the passages that refer to the Kingdom element in Paul's
preaching: "And he entered the synagogue and for three months
spoke boldly, arguing and pleading about the Kingdom of God. . . ."
Other passages include Acts 20:25; Romans 14:17; I Corinthians
4:20; I Thessalonians 1:5; Colossians 4:11; and Colossians 1:13.

Felder perhaps expresses the majority opinion about the preaching of Paul and social issues when he said "it should always be borne
in mind that Paul's preaching is determined by a dualistic, individu-
alistic and apocalyptic dynamic which only incidentally has relevance
for social justice."[11] Howard Thurman removes Paul from any consideration of having a genuine concern with social justice because of
his personal circumstances:

> Paul was a Jew, even as Jesus was a Jew. By blood, training, background, and
> religion he belonged to the Jewish minority. . . . But unlike them, for the most

---

[10]C. H. Dodd, *The Apostolic Preaching and its Developments* (London: Hodder and
Stoughton Limited, 1936) 19.

[11]Cane Hope Felder, "Preaching in the Ministry of Jesus."

part, he was a free Jew; he was a citizen of Rome. A desert and a sea were placed between his status in the empire and that of his fellow Jews.... He was of a minority but with majority privileges. If a Roman soldier in some prison in Asia Minor was taking advantage of him, he could make an appeal directly to Caesar....

Now Jesus was not a Roman citizen.... If a Roman soldier pushed Jesus into a ditch ... he would be just another Jew in the ditch.[12]

Some of the leaders of the early church exhibited social sensitivity at least to some extent.

(1) Clement's Exhortation to the Greeks and his sermon on the wealthy based on Mark 10:17-31 indicate this sensitivity. The Exhortation to the Greeks includes his statement on the Danger of Custom and Soldiers of Peace. In the former he decried custom as it "strangles man; it turns him away from truth; it leads him away from life; it is a snare, an abyss, a pit, a devouring evil."[13] Those who have been and are social victims are well aware that custom often plays a significant part in their victimization.

(2) In Tertullian's Apologetic and Practical Treatise social concern is expressed in the words: "We, therefore, who are united in mind and soul, doubt not about having our possessions in common. With us, all things are shared promiscuously, except our wives."[14]

(3) In Ambrose's *Letters* social sensitivity is expressed in the treatment of several topics. These include Rich Possessions, Caesar and God, Double Bondage, Nature of Liberty, Some Real Riches, and others.

(4) Social concerns are expressed in Augustine's cities: "The heavenly city, then, while it sojourns on earth, calls citizens out of all nations, and gathers together a society of pilgrims of all languages, not scrupling about diversities in the manners, laws, and institutions whereby earthly peace is secured and maintained but recognizing

---

[12]Howard Thurman, *Jesus and the Disinherited*, 32, 33.

[13]Stanley Irving Stuber, *The Christian Reader* (New York: Association Press, 1952) 32, 33.

[14]Ibid., 39.

that, however various these are, they all tend to one and the same end of earthly peace."[15]

It should be clear that preaching has addressed critical social issues during every era in the history of the faith. This has not always been the powerful prophetic preaching, however, which brings to bear the tenets, promises, and judgment of a great historic faith. Sometimes it has been feeble and anemic and ineffectual. There has never been a period, however, without prophetic voices being heard from within the faith addressing the issues.

Mention will be made here of the preaching that occurred during slavery, the social gospel preaching, especially as epitomized in the preaching of Walter Rauschenbusch, and the preaching of Mordecai Johnson and Benjamin Mays.

The preaching that was done during the period of formal slavery in the United States may be placed in four categories: (1) Abolitionist preaching; (2) preaching in support of slavery; (3) the preaching of slaves themselves; and (4) preaching that evaded the issue of slavery. The Baptists, Presbyterians, and Methodists were among the church denominations that split over the issue. All who broke the imposed silence on the issue and spoke from pulpits or elsewhere based their proclamations upon scripture, while some chose or felt compelled to refrain from speaking on slavery from the pulpits.

Theodore Parker and Henry Ward Beecher were among those who exerted great influence in opposing slavery as morally and spiritually untenable. It is reported that "slavery felt the full force of his [Parker's] prophetic condemnation" and that he exerted great political influence upon Sumner, Chase, and Lincoln.[16] In the front ranks of pulpit speakers who supported slavery were James H. Thornwell and William Swan Plumer.

Often overlooked in the consideration of the preaching that was done during slavery is that done by the slave preachers themselves. Many of these had been medicine men in Africa and, therefore, understood their responsibility for the physical as well as the spiritual

[15]Ibid., 78.

[16]DeWitte Holland, *Sermons in American History* (Nashville TN: Abingdon Press, 1971) 208.

well-being of their people. The sermons in condemnation of the institution of slavery offered hope for the downtrodden and gave them the incentive to set their hopes to music with such spirituals as:

> Didn't my Lord deliver Daniel?
> Then, why not *every* man?

and

> Go down, Moses, 'way down in Egypt land
> tell ole Phar'oh to let my people go!

The Social Gospel Movement was led by bold and courageous persons who made their social claims without hesitation. In an address at Andover Newton Theological School on the occasion of the fiftieth anniversary of the death of Walter Rauschenbusch, James M. Gufstafson referred to the uncommon boldness of Social Gospel leaders:

> Not only did they say forthrightly what they thought was wrong with American society, and what was needed to remove the social ills of the nation; they also were bold in the way in which they made claims. . . .[17]

Much is known about the thinking and work of Rauschenbusch as well as other leaders of the Social Gospel Movement. Yet little is known of the preaching of Rauschenbusch. Max Stackhouse has said that one really knows a theologian as well by his or her preaching as by his or her systematic reflections. The South African theologian, Allan Boesak, suggests that there is a certain vulnerability that comes along with preaching, which the theologian does not experience in theologizing in the "safe cubicle of theoretical contemplation."[18]

It has been charged that, while the reformers moved the focus of faith from the altar to the pulpit, Walter Rauschenbusch is responsible for the decline of the sermon. He did this by moving the focus of faith from the pulpit to the structures of life. This did not mean

---

[17]*The Andover Newton Quarterly*, 1969.

[18]Allan Boesak, *The Finger of God* (Maryknoll NY: Orbis Books, 1982) xi.

that he intended to cause a decline in preaching. During his day, Rauschenbusch was known for his preaching. When the Social Gospel leader made the pilgrimage from conservative piety to social radicalism, the primary emphasis in his sermons moved from holiness to righteousness. It is interesting that the social emphasis was usually present in the sermon that he delivered in the evenings. The reasons for this are not clear.

Something of Walter Rauschenbusch's concept of the preacher as proclaimer of the relevant gospel in socially critical times is seen in a sermon he delivered on Hebrews 11:24-26: "By faith, Moses, when grown up, refused to be called a son of the daughter of Pharaoh, choosing rather to suffer the afflictions with the people of God." Here are some of the points he made about Moses in the sermon:

He could have had a life of luxury. . . .

He could have had a better life of knowledge. The wisdom of Egyptians was the greatest in the world. . . .

He could have had a life of power. There was depression of the many and the rapid rise of the few. . . .

> The text says he refused it all. Not only that, but he chose what was just the opposite. Imagine some Southern planter stepping out and becoming a slave in the cotton field. National degradation stings the high-souled man. Israel was trampled by the whip of the task master falling on their backs. Their condition was one of poverty and poor food and poor living conditions. People were in ignorance. He must have felt repelled. And he joined the downtrodden and the lost cause. He chose the solitude of a leader. Perhaps he did not see the splendor of this success. He made a nation of slave bricklayers. It was the greatest challenge of the ancient world. The actuating cause was "faith." He pitted faith against evidence; spiritual against the temporal, the future against the present. That requires faith.

Among the reasons this sermon is important in the present consideration is the fact that Walter Rauschenbusch presents here his role definition of the preacher. The priorities, the sacrifices that Moses made represent the kind of action in which the preacher must engage. Social crisis preaching for Rauschenbusch was not merely a matter of the proclamation of the Word, though that was vital. It was surrounding that proclamation with a life that participates with God in correcting social evils and institutes social justice.

It must be mentioned that the Social Gospel Movement did not rise to the occasion in the face of serious racial problems in the United States. While some few, almost passing, references to the problem were made by Social Gospel leaders, the words were at times intensely weak and often inaudible. Jean Russell charges that

> The most remarkable period of unconcern about race relations in the history of American Protestantism is that period when the Social Gospel Movement was at its zenith.[19]

In relation to Rauschenbusch himself she said: "Rauschenbusch's statements on race were marred by uncertainty and feebleness and sometimes revealed a racial bias."[20] While acknowledging that Rauschenbusch did express concern for the racial problem at times, this was not as definitive as were his positions on other issues. In a booklet, which he published as a basis for Christian concern with racial issues, Rauschenbusch "offered no guidance to ministers who might have been concerned about widespread rioting and lynching . . ."[21] The historical perspective provides a basis for deep gratitude that such proclaimers of the Word as Walter Rauschenbusch carried on their ministries and provided such a potent basis for many others who came later. For example, Charles D. Hubert, late dean of the department of religion at Morehouse College, was the first Black person exposed to the Social Gospel. He instilled its principles in the generations of students and parishioners who sat at his feet. At the same time, that perspective is a reminder that even those who assign to themselves the distinction of being particularly concerned with social issues are morally vulnerable and, more than likely, are guilty. Social offenses are perpetrated by those to the left as well as those to the right. Indeed, some of the worst offenders are those on the left because they are often not sensitive to the possibility that they could offend, and assume the posture of the Pharisee in the temple who said, "I thank thee, Lord, that I am not as others are."

---

[19] Jean Russell, *God's Lost Cause* (Valley Forge PA: Judson Press, 1969) 70.

[20] Ibid., 82.

[21] Ibid., 83.

Social victims tend to produce the most persuasive and consistent social crisis preaching. This is not to discount those who stand outside a certain experiential realm, but who are among those rare individuals who do identify with social victims in a meaningful way. Perhaps most of the sermons delivered by women and Blacks in the United States are based on the understanding that liberation is the content of the Christian gospel and that God has a bias in the direction of those who are oppressed. The sermons included in Justo González' *Proclaiming the Acceptable Year* are brilliant and prophetic sermons presented in the main by social victims in the United States and in other lands. Boesak's *The Finger of God* presents the liberation theology of a Black South African in sermon form. Two decades ago, Alfred T. Davies combined the sermons of social victims with those of other concerned and committed preachers in *The Pulpit Speaks on Race*.

The preaching of social victims deserves more time and space than can be provided here. In fact, it would not have been inappropriate for this entire series to have been devoted to "The Preaching of Social Victims," for there is much to be learned from them. By this is not meant persons who at the moment are caught up in a particular crisis. Rather, the reference is to persons who are identified with an oppressed group and whose day-to-day experiences must include addressing social issues.

Mordecai Wyatt Johnson was described by Marcus Boulware as one whose "language tends to be lively, descriptive, and erudite. . . . The audience feels his ideas surge forth with the power of a jet airliner. His persuasion is strong and convincing. He is a natural verbal artist when he describes the origin of racial prejudice between the slaves and poor whites who scarcely eked out a living from the mountain hills of the South. . . . The orator arouses positively hysterical enthusiasm by his arguments in behalf of the downtrodden."[22] It was clear to all who heard Dr. Johnson speak that he was a preacher and that his addresses were often sermons. He had served as pastor of the

---

[22]Marcus Hanna Boulware, *The Oratory of Negro Leaders: 1900-1968* (Westport CT: Negro Universities Press, 1969) 72-73.

First Baptist Church of Charleston, West Virginia, and for many years was president of Howard University in Washington, D. C.

Benjamin Elijah Mays served as pastor of only one church, but his speaking was obviously that of a brilliant minister who had made a life commitment to the resolution of some of the social problems that plagued Black people. His doctorate from the University of Chicago was in the field of theology, but his major interest has been and is in the field of education. For many years he was president of Morehouse College in Atlanta, Georgia, and subsequent to that time, he was president of the Atlanta School Board. His preaching has been before religious conventions, churches, academic audiences, and especially the generations of students at Morehouse College. His sermons usually interpreted the social scene from the perspective of high moral standards and what can be accomplished by the oppressed through aggressive action and dogged determination. His preaching has been characteristically dressed in the appealing clothes of eloquence.

Martin Luther King, Jr., one of the most effective social crisis preachers of the twentieth century, was profoundly influenced by Johnson and Mays. He will be discussed later.

History is replete with the powerful and influential preaching of numerous other persons who understood and assumed their social responsibility in the proclamation of the Word.

Whether heralded or unheralded; whether acclaimed or unacclaimed; whether heeded or unheeded, during every period of Jewish and Christian history there have been persistent, prophetic voices that have proclaimed the Word with all its social impact and power.

BIBLICAL PERSPECTIVE

The entire preaching enterprise must be seen in Biblical perspective. This is imperative for all social crisis preaching. Among the reasons for this are the following: (1) The Bible is a "mirror" for the believing community; thus, as James A. Sanders has said, those caught in contemporary tensions can see themselves reflected in tensions as depicted in the Bible; (2) the Bible is a source for social crisis preaching; (3) the Bible is often used as an instrument of oppression; it is therefore important that more of the enlightened perspective be presented and acted upon; (4) throughout the Bible there is demonstrated a special concern for those who are victimized by adverse social, political, and economic conditions.

Much of the proclamation that occurs within the pages of the Bible may be categorized as social crisis proclamation of the prophets, of Jesus himself, and of the apostles. Gardner C. Taylor sees the Bible as adding color and imagination to otherwise dull preaching:

> ... too much preaching ... is too horizontal, too colorless, too unimaginative. Much of this can be overcome if those who preach would catch the sounds and sights and smells of the accounts recorded.[23]

In order to accomplish this, Taylor contends, the preacher must transcend a mere intellectual approach to the scriptures, but must open her or his whole being to the Word. "We must not forego reading and listening to comprehend what the Bible is saying in our own lives."[24]

The Old Testament prophets have long since been seen as quasi-models for Christian social crisis preaching, for they were ever relating social and political well-being to religion in their preaching. In fact, Von Rad suggests that among the elements present in the circumstances out of which they emerged were those that were social, economic, and political:

> ... the emergence of the prophets is very closely connected with four data all prepared long in advance. The degeneracy of Jahwism because of syncretism. ... The second was of a political nature, the systematic emancipation from Jahweh which is offered, due to the formation of the state. Through her armaments and her alliance—in a word, through her political tactics—Israel had thrown off Jahweh's guiding hand and become politically autonomous. The third cause lay in the economic and social developments which both kingdoms had undergone.[25]

---

[23]Gardner C. Taylor, *How Shall They Preach* (Elgin IL: Progressive Baptist Publishing House, 1977) 60.

[24]Ibid., 60.

[25]Gerhard von Rad, *Old Testament Theology*, vol. 1 (New York: Armstrong, 1902) 1-12.

The fourth cause was the rise of Assyria. The clear suggestion here is that the rise of the prophets was in a measure a response to the political, economic, and social state of affairs.

The scorching denunciations and proclamations of some of the prophets were made in the interest of encouraging adherence to divine law. At the same time, they were concerned with social, political, and economic issues in a major way. Divine law required justice and compassion for the oppressed, and prophecy apart from or contradictory to this emphasis raised serious questions regarding the genuineness of the prophet. No one can read the Old Testament and especially the prophets without receiving the clear impression that these rugged forthtellers represented a God who was profoundly concerned with social issues and one who has definite bias in the direction of the oppressed.

J. A. Broadus, the 1899 Lyman Beecher lecturer, characterizes the work of the prophets as that of reminding the people of their sins; exhorting them to repent; and instructing them in religious, moral, *social*, and personal duties.[26] Here again the social dimension of their function is seen in conjunction with the call for repentance and adherence to the laws of God. When they predicted a dire future and called for moral action on the political front, this was not a departure from the theme of repentance for sins: "These proclamations are, of course, by no means just the result of an intelligent estimate of the political situation, for they designate this threatened disaster as one brought about by Jahweh to punish the sins of his people."[27]

According to the report in the Gospel of Luke, Jesus began his preaching ministry with the startling declaration that his would be a scripture-based, spirit-directed social ministry.

> The Spirit of the Lord is upon me,
> because he has anointed me to preach goodness to the poor,
> He has sent me to proclaim release to the captive
> and recovering of sight to the blind,
> to set at liberty those who are oppressed,

---

[26]John A. Broadus, *Lectures on the History of Preaching* (New York: Armstrong, 1902) 1-12.

[27]Von Rad, *Old Testament Theology*, 1:66,67.

to proclaim the acceptable year of the Lord.

—Luke 4:18, 19

The theme of Jesus' preaching is presented in Mark 1:15: "The time is fulfilled, and the Kingdom of God is at hand; repent, and believe the gospel." He placed major emphasis upon the Kingdom of God and issues that pertained to that kingdom. The Kingdom of God is both a present reality and a future hope. It simply means the kingly rule or the sovereignty of God. And, incidentally, the more chaotic a situation or an era is, the more relevant is the notion of the sovereignty of God. Thus, periods of intense social crisis may concretize the meaning of the Kingdom of God with its emphasis upon God's sovereignty. The social and political implications of the Kingdom of God are clear. In fact, the very words used to describe this major emphasis in the preaching of Jesus call to mind a politically organized community or major territorial unit having a monarchical form of government headed by a king or queen. The Kingdom of God is the kingly rule of a God who is biased in the direction of the oppressed. The coming of the Kingdom has social and political meaning which cannot appropriately be disregarded. Gustavo Gutierrez calls attention to the fact that "The struggle for a just world in which there is no oppression, servitude, or alienated work will signify the coming of the kingdom. The kingdom and injustice are incompatible."[28] Smith and Zepp contend that for Martin Luther King, Jr. the "beloved community" and the Kingdom of God were synonymous terms:

> Although the doctrine of the Kingdom of God did not occupy an explicit place in King's writings, it was obviously implicit in everything he said and did. The explanation for the lack of prominence of this doctrine undoubtedly lies in the fact that the kingdom of God and the Beloved Community were synonymous in King's thought.[29]

King said explicitly, however, that "The Kingdom of God will be a

---

[28]Gustavo Gutierrez, *A Theology of Liberation* (Maryknoll NY: Orbis Books, 1973) 168.

[29]Kenneth L. Smith and Ira G. Zepp, Jr. *Search for the Beloved Community: The Thinking of Martin Luther King, Jr.* (Valley Forge PA: Judson Press, 1974) 129.

society in which men and women live as children of God should live. It will be a kingdom controlled by the law of love...."[30]

The words of Jesus himself regarding the Kingdom are of greatest value in terms of the nature and meaning of the kingdom as central to his preaching.

Jesus' own words and the context of those words indicate the nature of the kingdom includes that which is social. The poor in spirit are blessed and the kingdom of heaven (or of God) belongs to them (Matthew 5:3). In the Lukan version of the Sermon on the Mount, reference is not made to the poor "in spirit," but rather to the poor: "Blessed are you poor, for yours is the Kingdom of God" (Luke 6:20). The place of social outcasts in the Kingdom is shown in Matthew 21:31, "Truly, I say to you, tax collectors and the harlots go into the Kingdom of God before you." Entrance to the kingdom will be a problem of special dimensions for the rich: "Again, I tell you, it is easier for a camel to go through the eye of a needle than for a rich man to enter the Kingdom of God" (Matthew 19:24).

Apostolic preaching heralded a new day for the proclamation of the Word of God. For one thing, it represented a time when the Kingdom of God had come. This was the meaning of the sermon that Peter delivered on the day of Pentecost. This must also be seen as an extremely important episode in terms of social concerns. Implicit in this experience is that which attacks (or transcends) serious social problems: cultural differences are transcended; ageism is addressed in the quotation from Joel which assigns vital responsibilities to the young *and* to the old; sexism is transcended with the words "your sons and daughters" will prophesy (Acts 2:5ff). Peter's sermon affirms fulfillment of the prophets' promises of a new type of society on earth. Holland characterizes the preaching of Peter as forthright and urgent, "using characteristic Hebrew style with vigorous verbs, concrete illustrations, and a minimum of abstractions."[31]

The record of the Word of God as found in scripture and proclamation of the Word must become one in order for that proclamation to attain its potential. Although at the outset of the sermon prepa-

---

[30]Ibid.

[31]Holland, *Sermons in American History*, 19.

ration process these appear as two separate entities, the ideal is that they come across as one even as separate ingredients are brought together to create a delectable dish. This is more easily said than done. Often the preacher himself/herself tries to force one upon the other when they seem not to be entirely compatible. In order for the Word of God to become present to generations other than those with whom that Word was originally identified, there are some gaps that must be bridged. Or, better, there are some relationships that must be demonstrated.

The proclamation of the Word must demonstrate the relationship between experience and exegesis. Homiletics textbooks give careful attention to the importance and process of exegesis, but rarely is the function of experience taken into account in these works. Experience can function negatively or positively in terms of eliciting the basic meaning of a scripture text and in the proclamation of the Word. In commenting on Juan Luis Segundo's notion of ideological suspicion, the Gonzálezes address the issue of the function of experience. They point to the fact that the experience of oppression often led to conclusions and concerns contrary to those represented by tradition as being "Christian" and "Biblical." The consequence was that some of the oppressed "opted for the movement and abandoned the church, while others did the opposite."[32] Many processes of exegesis inferentially recommend the discounting of experience as a hermeneutical category. Yet, it is historically validated that persons who experience oppression are more likely to comprehend and identify with the Word of God in scripture than those external to that experience. Keck says, "it appears that for most creative interpreters the meaning of the text seems somewhat self-evident because that meaning is found by discernment and insight rather than by applying principles or following rules of interpretation."[33] Here the experiences of the interpreter are urgent.

Miles Jones, distinguished pastor-scholar and homiletician, contends that exegesis that disregards the category of experience pro-

---

[32]Justo González and Catherine González, *Liberation Preaching* (Nashville: Abingdon Press, 1980) 32.

[33]Leander E. Keck, *The Bible in the Pulpit: The Renewal of Biblical Preaching* (Nashville: Abingdon Press, 1978) 113.

duces "flat facts and sterile statements." Experience is a valid force
through which scripture is heard:

> Reliance upon so-called scholarship seems to distrust experience as a voice
> through which Scripture is heard. Perhaps that is why the Black preaching
> tradition has seemed to some of its critics to care very little for many of these
> learned considerations and has tended, for the most part, to march on
> through the decades unaffected by the "mainstream mouthings" of Ameri-
> can preaching. Of course . . . the Black preaching tradition does not despise
> scholarship . . . Perhaps that daring to trust experience perspective is why the
> best in oral culture of Black America from anecdotes to folklore has been pre-
> served in its preaching. . . . (The Black Church tradition) takes seriously the
> tension between the static scripture and the flow of fellowship . . . The
> preacher and parishioner take part in what is proclaimed, not by contrived
> "dialogue," but by the evoking of sentient expressions of shared
> experiences.[34]

The experiential orientation of the oppressed provides an irreplaceable aid in the interpretation of scripture. The Word of God becomes
present in that situation through the experiences of the oppressed
incorporated in the exegesis basic to the proclamation of the Word.
When *that* Word is proclaimed, the oppressed become aware that
God's communication is not only to them, but is on their behalf in a
major way.

The question may be raised as to the hermeneutical relevance of
the experiences of those who are not among the oppressed. Of
course, their experiences also inform and condition interpretation.
This is the problem to which the Gonzálezes refer. Experiences that
run counter to the direction in which the record of the Word of God
moves must be transcended. The Segundo ideological suspicion may
be applied. It must be remembered that the authentic essence of the
Christian faith champions the cause of the oppressed. This is basic in
any approach to scripture. Experience can affirm, refute, illustrate,
contradict, illumine, contrast, and the like.

*The proclamation of the Word must demonstrate the relationship between
extra-biblical tradition and the Word of God in scripture.* It is clear that this
is dangerous ground because of the presence again of emotional land

---

[34]Personal letter from Miles J. Jones to Kelly Miller Smith dated 27 January
1982.

mines. This is basically because much of religious tradition claims to be scripture-based, however unsupportable these claims may be. In some cases the eisegetical feats involved here are amazing. Often, denominational and social dogma dictate theological and ecclesiological claims far more forcefully than exegetical integrity.

The preacher, in deference to the dogmatic context and demands, is often tempted to "make" a scripture text where there is none. For example, some years ago a popular preacher was invited to deliver a doctrinal sermon before a large Baptist group. He used as a scripture text Mark 1:4 and spoke from the subject "The Wilderness Baptist Preacher." He posited the favorite denominational claims in that passage of scripture. To be sure, there are those who are more sophisticated in their dogmatic eisegeses, but the offense is not thereby lessened.

The present concern is with the relationship between scripture from which preachers derive texts, and the like, and sectarian and social dogma or tradition. In exploring this relationship it would not be appropriate to blandly place all extra-biblical tradition in the "liability" column and all scripture in the "assets" column. While the dynamic Word of God may be revealed anyplace—including in extra-biblical tradition—it does not appear on every single page of the Bible.

It is true that denominational pioneers have not always listened for the Word of God before they staked their claims. Similarly, those who are wedded to certain social customs have not always done a careful study of scripture before pursuing a given course of action. H. R. Niebuhr and others have called attention to the propensity to assign scriptural support for their positions, each espousing a notion of the authority of the scriptures.

It is interesting that racial divisions of churches were until recently built into their dogma, especially among White churches. "The dogma which divides the racial churches is . . . not theological," Niebuhr points out, ". . . the White churches . . . have incorporated it in their popular theology and sought to provide a biblical base for it." (In another sense it has been charged that the racial problems in the United States are rooted in historical theology. Jean Russell, in *God's Lost Cause*, views the various theological movements as bearing primary blame for racial conditions in the United States.)

To suggest that extra-biblical tradition has at least the status of scripture in some instances is to raise the vital questions of the authority of scripture. To be sure, there are times when denominational or social dogma is more compelling in determining the direction of a sermon than scripture, contentions to the contrary notwithstanding. This means that extra-biblical tradition is accorded an authority which, in that instance, transcends that of scripture. This does not prima facie signal that tradition has authority that transcends that of the Word of God. Indeed, the word of tradition may be received as the Word of God is received, although it may not be basically theological in content. It must be recalled, however, that the Word of God is God's communication with members of the human family and it has at least the following characteristics: (1) it is for those "whose backs are against the wall";[35] (2) it "inaugurates a new age in which all oppressed people become his people";[36] (3) it is God's initiative in divine to human communication; (4) it is good news for the disinherited and the dispossessed. The authority of the Word of God is the authority of God; the authority of the Bible is the same to the extent that it contains a record of the Word of God containing the above characteristics.

Preaching must demonstrate the relationship between exegesis and proclamation. There is no question that careful exegesis is important for social crisis preaching in particular. The Bible is irreplaceably important for those who would address the social problems that plague the present generation. It is folly to speak of using scripture in this manner without recognizing that sound interpretation is essential. The preacher usually understands what must be done in the study. The question arises as to how to get from the study to the pulpit without making the latter appear to be the former. Leander Keck warns of the temptation to deliver a ten-minute lecture on the passage of scripture and a ten-minute sermon, neither of which will be adequate.

An experienced preacher once told a group of seminary students that if you are going to prepare biscuits for dinner guests, it is not nec-

---

[35]Howard Thurman, *Jesus and the Disinherited*, 112.
[36]James H. Cone, *Black Theology and Black Power*, 69.

essary to place the flour bag, salt, shortening, baking powder, and so forth, on the table. Simply make good biscuits and the guests will know that the proper ingredients are included. (A recognized problem with the illustration: who makes biscuits this way these days—when ready-made rolls are so readily available?) The point, however, is that there is the temptation on the part of some preachers to parade their Hebrew and Greek before the people as evidence of adequate preparation or academic status. The challenge for the preacher is to use all of the help he or she can get in the preparation of the sermon. When proclamation time comes, the preacher is challenged to present the simple gospel with all of its power. The quality of the sermon must demonstrate that the preaching task is taken seriously.

It should be noted that determining the social context of biblical texts offers help and safeguards. When the social setting of prophetic proclamation is seen clearly, one is also able to distinguish between that which is fundamental truth and power in that or any social context. The gap between exegesis and proclamation is thus narrowed.

The emphasis here has been that preaching is an effective way of addressing critical social issues. While this must not be the sole action taken by the minister, it is vitally important and can yield desired results. The kind of preaching most appropriate for this endeavor is biblical preaching. It has been recalled that Leander Keck is right in the contention that biblical preaching is not always as simple as some would suggest. It lends itself to all kinds of atrocities and distortions. When social crisis preaching is done biblically, it must be mindful of the precedent set in the preaching of the prophets, Jesus of Nazareth, and the Apostles. It must be done in such a manner to demonstrate the relationship between experience and exegesis, between extra-biblical tradition and the Word of God in scripture, and between exegesis and proclamation. The work is not likely to be easy, but it will be rewarding.

David Buttrick suggests that six questions should be asked in the effort to accomplish proper use of scripture:

(1) What is the form? That is to say, is the passage poetry, public address, or story. This question must deal not only with the identification of the form, but also with the reason for its use.

(2) What is the plot, structure or shape?

(3) What is the field of concern?

(4) What is the logic movement?

(5) What is the addressed world?

(6) What is the passage trying to do?

One suggests that added to that should be the Gonzálezes' point that those attempting to interpret the scriptures should ask the political question. Traditional interpretations of the Bible generally are biased against the oppressed. When the use of the Bible is done in such a manner that the Bible speaks for itself, it then becomes clear that the Word of God in scripture is supportive of the oppressed.

BLACK PERSPECTIVE

The suggestion has already been advanced that most of the preaching done by Blacks and women in the United States is likely to be based on the view that liberation is the content of the Christian gospel. This understanding of the gospel is important for these particular preachers because they are constantly having to address critical social issues both sermonically and otherwise. Because of their own experiences of oppression they find solace and encouragement in the understanding that the Christian gospel is concerned with their plight in a major way.

The preaching of Blacks has been heralded, criticized, ridiculed, misunderstood, extolled since the days of formal slavery. More often than not, this preaching has been concerned with critical social issues, although at times it has appeared to have been concerned with other issues only. Beneath the surface of almost any Black preaching is the theme of Black oppression and Black liberation. In order to take this brief glance at social crisis preaching in Black perspective it is essential to take into account the ecclesiastical context in which this preaching occurs, the Black social crisis preacher as leader, the trans-denominational response to social crises, and the Black social crisis sermon itself.

The Black church was born as a protest movement. Its initial purpose was to address the problems that victimized Black people. These problems presented themselves not only in society generally, but also in the churches. It became clear early on that the attitudes that prevailed in larger society also prevailed in the churches. Segregation, Kyle Haselden points out, existed in the churches of New York City before it existed in the bus and railroad stations of the South. There is no wonder, then, that Black church groups separated themselves from such churches in order to form their own churches and denominations.

The Black church in America not only provides the care necessary for those wounded in the fray; it also provides the experience of liberation itself for an oppressed people. Moreover, it provides a setting for the redress of grievances and for the addressing of problems that exist. Often, the addressing of these problems takes the form of sermons. It does not mean that the preacher is evading taking the message to those who are guilty; it means, rather, that the message is being presented to the audience to which the Black preacher has immediate access. It is true, however, that some of the Black preachers were welcome to preach during slavery and afterwards as long as their preaching did not get "out of hand."

The social crisis preacher who is Black is usually more than a pulpiteer. He or she is also usually a community activist. The preacher of the social conscious gospel is also a leader of the community. The Black community usually expects the Black preacher to be a leader of social movements or at least to be a staunch supporter.

Some of these leaders understand it to be their responsibility to do only that which pertains to his or her particular congregation. Also, there are social crisis proclaimers who feel that their functioning in the community must be only as pastor of this or that church— not as leader of a given movement.

Since the mid-sixties there have been efforts to form organizations that go beyond denominational boundaries in order to meet the crises that existed at a given time. The National Conference of Black Christians was formed in 1966 in order to demonstrate that Black power was not contrary to the Christian gospel but is affirmed by that gospel. Other organizations that transcend denominational barriers in order to fulfill a social ministry include: the Southern Christian Leadership Conference; Operation PUSH; the Congress of National Black Churches and the National Black Pastors Conference.

The social crisis sermon is usually structured in the festive manner that characterizes much of Black preaching. In spite of the fact that the preacher is dealing with a critical issue, there is often a mood of celebration and victory in the sermons. The Black social crisis sermon usually exhibits the three sermon qualities that Goethe suggests: proving—to appeal to the reason; painting—to appeal to the imagination; and persuading—to appeal to the heart. The Black sermon is dialogically presented because members of the congregation can usually completely identify with the matter being presented.

It is important to realize that there is no monolithic Black preaching nor Black preacher. The variety is dramatic at times.

The preaching of Dr. Martin Luther King, Jr. represents social crisis preaching at its best. Marcus Boulware stated that the speaking of Martin Luther King, Jr., "seared the American Conscience." While many would agree that the searing was not deep enough, it cannot be denied that the foremost speaker on critical social issues of the last half of the twentieth century was Dr. King.

Zepp and Smith notwithstanding, Martin Luther King was a product of the Black church. As C. Eric Lincoln said, "He belonged to the Black church, and in it and for it he lived and died. It was Martin Luther King, Jr. who made the Black church aware of its power to effect change . . . King . . . was the first to put together a sustained coalition of Christian leadership at the pulpit level."[37] It is true, then, that King was not only an outstanding speaker on critical social issues; he was an incomparable leader in the direction of resolution of the issues.

The preaching of Martin Luther King was usually scripture-based, but he called on many other resources relevant for the topic at hand. His sermons were consistent in that they were reflective of his theological posture and social commitment. As is evident from every sermon or address he delivered, King gave great attention to the importance of preparation. L. D. Reddick in *Crusader Without Violence* said that King "likes to read up on his topic for a couple of days, outline it, then write what he wants to say. He will then lay the manuscript aside, going back to it a few hours before it is delivered. When he has gone through this process, he does not need to use either script or notes when he stands up to make a speech."[38] As is well known, King

---

[37]C. Eric Lincoln, *The Black Church Since Frazier* (New York: Schocken Books, 1977) 114-15.

[38]L. D. Reddick, *Crusader Without Violence* (New York: Harper and Brothers, 1959) 11.

seldom used a manuscript. In his presentation he used his rich trombone-like voice to great advantage. In the sermons of King the ingredients of scripture, extra-biblical sources, results of personal reflection, illustration of scripture, and the like, all come together into an exciting whole without becoming the V-8 juice appropriately decried by Leander Keck. His preaching combines unmistakable commitment, intellectual competency, artistic language and content design, effective voice use, and clear objective.

Martin Luther King was and remains the dominant religious personage of the twentieth century. His social crisis message was not only communicated through the uncommon power of his well-chosen and eloquent words; his very presence communicated a message that depicted the essence of the Christian faith. Since there was such a blending of words and work on the part of King, it would be inappropriate to speak of his preaching apart from his service. No mere recital of a few of his accomplishments can exhaust the meaning of King any more than a timepiece can measure the length of eternity. Yet, the picture may be enhanced by the listing of a few:

(1) He placed the struggle for human dignity and justice within the proper moral context.

(2) He added the dimension of direct action to the legal justice thrust in the effort to attain human rights.

(3) He was the first to involve the masses in the struggle for Black emancipation.

(4) He involved religious leaders and institutions in the movement for human rights in an especially courageous and different way.

(5) His philosophy and action not only exhibited great courage on his part, but called forth uncommon courage and fearlessness on the part of others.

(6) He established heretofore unknown alliances in the effort to attain human rights. These included persons of diverse religious, ethnic, racial, educational, political, and economic backgrounds.

(7) Perhaps partially because of his own intellectual training he involved intellectuals and educators in the struggle for human rights in an unprecedented way.

(8) In forming the Southern Christian Leadership Conference he mounted the first organized Southern-based mass attack on the racist patterns of the South.

(9) He caused vital civil rights legislation to be enacted.

(10) He led the first serious assault on Northern racism.

Perhaps more than anyone else of the present era, Martin Luther King calls this generation to creative, effective, and persistent social ministry. This ministry cannot be accomplished simply by agitation to make his birthday a national holiday, as important as that would be for the soul of America. This ministry must be carried out through the proclamation of the uncompromising Word of a caring God and through the concrete courageous action required by that Word.

IV
PROCLAMATION
AND BEYOND

*So they called them and charged them not to speak or
teach at all in the name of Jesus. But Peter and John
answered them, "Whether it is right in the sight of God
to listen to you rather than to God, you must judge; for
we cannot but speak of what we have seen and heard."*
ACTS 4:18-20

The social crisis sermon is never properly a museum piece of social oratory. Nor is it appropriately an animated discussion of current social issues. Rather, it is a call to action. It is preaching on the highest order. It is quality preaching. There can be no quality preaching that does not take into account this major thrust of the Word of God as found in scripture. There can be no effective and proper preaching on social crises that does not adhere to the basic requirements of quality preaching. Quality preaching is the efficacious proclamation of the genuine Word of God. It is adherence to the mandate found in 2 Timothy 4:2: "preach the word, be urgent in season and out of season, convince, rebuke and exhort, be unfailing in patience and in teaching."

The preconditions for social crisis preaching have been discussed. Under the caption of "Purview," the terrain was observed in order to see its composition. Questions were asked as to what and where the danger points are and what can be learned of the topography.

The discussion of "Purview" led to a consideration of the importance of "Perception" for the entire enterprise. That discussion centered in two foci: (1) how should the socially relevant Word of God be perceived by the preacher? and (2) how should it be perceived by the congregation? We contended that the preacher has the responsibility of bridging the gap between perception and reality. This process is aided by the raising of pertinent questions regarding the task and the congregation in the quest for clarity. On the topic "Perspective" we showed that any entity is seen more clearly when it is viewed from the perspective of other illumining realities. Not only does this effort at seeing social crisis preaching in perspective reveal different ways of looking at it; it also makes clearer what social crisis preaching truly is. Without an adequate perspective, what is seen is largely false because the part is mistaken for the whole. This arduous responsibility of addressing critical social issues through the sermon calls for the best possible efforts on the part of the preacher.

Any attempt to do social crisis preaching by ignoring historical, biblical, and Black perspectives is disastrous. Yet, mere notice of them in the preparatory process is not sufficient. Surveying, perceiving, and viewing in perspective are not the end. Rather, that end is *kerygma*—proclamation. It is communication. It is "telling the story." But, even this is not the *final* end. The critical question has to do with what comes after proclamation takes place. It must be recalled that social crisis preaching is preaching for a decision—*for Christ*.

All of these considerations come together for the proclamation of the Word. In pursuit of the present topic, several matters must be taken into account: (1) the "pre-proclamation, pre-crisis" function of the preacher; (2) the content; (3) the words used; (4) the perceptual powers of focus; (5) the structure; (6) delivery of the social crisis sermon; and (7) the post-delivery function of the preacher.

"PRE-PROCLAMATION" FUNCTION
OF THE PREACHER

Effective proclamation is greatly dependent upon what the function of the preacher has been prior to the crisis proclamation. Communication is facilitated by the consistent function of the minister in the direction of justice and liberation of the oppressed. When members of the congregation understand that their minister is usually on the cutting edge of constructive change, the crisis proclamation delivered at the time of a particular crisis will be expected and generally well received. It should be clear that if the sermon is the minister's first and only indication of concern, there is likely to be difficulty in getting the message across. Communication actually begins not when the text and the sermon title are announced, but when the minister functions in the community in relation to critical social circumstances and shows social sensitivity prior to proclamation.

Social crises are the day-to-day experience of those who minister to social victims. Those whose ministries are not among social victims have the following peculiar responsibilities in this regard:

(1) Encouraging the congregations over which they preside to welcome into their membership all persons regardless of their race, national origin, socioeconomic status, educational achievement, and the like.

(2) Giving consistent attention to social concerns before they reach crisis proportions.

(3) Acquainting the congregation with enlightened pronouncements and documents produced by their denominations as well as those of others that address social concerns from within the context of the Christian faith.

(4) Embarking upon periods of study that point out the urgent contemporary social issues even before they have reached crisis proportions.

(5) Reflecting in their preaching an understanding of the social relevance of the Christian gospel before a specific crisis arises.

DEVELOPMENT OF CONTENT

Howard Thurman reported that his homiletics teacher in seminary once told the class they were not required to deliver great sermons each time they stood in the pulpit, but they were expected to wrestle with a great idea each time they stood there. What is the big idea? It is a valid question to raise about preaching. Remember the George Bernard Shaw depiction of some preaching being like seltzer water—a big fuss over nothing. The preaching enterprise is in some measure of trouble when the trappings of preaching—eloquence, scholarship, voice control, and so forth, are more in evidence than the "big idea" being presented and with which the preacher is wrestling.

It should be clear that social crisis preaching is not merely a report on some social circumstances or the expression of an opinion regarding that situation. Of course, this may well be involved in the presentation of the social crisis sermon, but it is far from all. The commentary that the preacher offers on the crisis must be based upon some idea. The question is this: what is the source of the idea and what, in fact, is the idea itself?

Henry Grady Davis has suggested that, structurally, the idea emerges as a response to the question, "What is the preacher saying about the subject?" In the case of social crisis preaching, the minister may have made it clear that she or he will be dealing with the race problem, for instance. That is the subject. That answers the question, What is the preacher talking about? Of greater importance is the second question. There is a broad range of possibilities as to what may be said *about* the subject. To be sure, the idea determines the form or structure of the sermon. Prior to that in importance, however, is the question of what the idea is. Does the idea of the preacher harmonize with the Word of God or is it simply an echo of the voice of society? If the idea is in harmony with the Word of God, then it will be on the side of the social victims. James Earl Massey puts the matter this way: "The sermon is the development of a theme growing out of an idea that focuses on a human issue or divine claim. The idea is the germ of the message, the theme forecasts the direction of the message, and the sermon is the full plan to address and involve the hearer in the idea."[1] The idea must be rooted in an expression of God's concern for some human condition. Of course, the Word of God in scripture is the most logical source of the ideas upon which sermons are based.

An idea is an entity (such as a thought, concept, sensation, or image) actually or potentially present to the consciousness. It is the central meaning or chief end of a particular situation or action. Unfortunately, people do not always feel a great need for ideas—either of their own or those of their minister. How easy it is for those who listen to preaching to comment favorably and even enthusiastically on the greatness of a given sermon without the slightest notion of what it was about. Some ministers have the capacity and the inclination to deliver sermons in such a manner as to win acclaim for themselves without bothering to have a central idea.

In the case of social crises, the idea is present prior to the crisis and provides direction for thinking and action during or with regard to

---

[1] James Earl Massey, *Designing the Sermon* (Nashville TN: Abingdon Press, 1980) 31.

the crisis. When the idea is derived from the Word of God in scripture or when it harmonizes with that Word, the preacher's sermon and action will reveal that relation and will be supportive of the social victims. Massey suggests that the sermon itself develops from an idea that focuses on a human issue *or* divine claim, but in a more precise sense the human issue and the divine claim are not separate. The whole point of social crisis preaching is the idea that God is concerned about human issues. This is the essence of the biblical message.

WORDS, WORD, WORDS

The idea that the social crisis sermon must be put into words for speech is the primary form of preaching. Job's reflection is apt: "How forcible are right words" (Job 6:25). Herbert Gezork tells of his experiences with the use of words when he first arrived in the United States from Germany. He said that he was guest minister at a German-American church in which the announcements, though strangely not the sermons, were done in English and German. He announced in German that the young people of the church were invited to a moonlight picnic. When he translated the announcement into English it came out, "The young people are invited to a 'moonshine party!' " The use of words is a vital consideration.

The preacher has the awesome responsibility of using words to proclaim the Word of God. Words are at times imprecise and freighted with meanings contrary to what may be intended. Sometimes they are, as Rudyard Kipling once said, "the most powerful drug used by humankind." The Word of God is God's communication with the human family. It is the sure defense of the oppressed. Yet, it must be conveyed by fragile words. In the Proverbs it is stated that "a word fitly spoken is like apples of gold in pictures of silver" (Proverbs 25:11), but what of the word that is not fitly spoken? When the Word of God is filtered through carelessly chosen and inappropriately spoken words, the power of that word is negated and its potential is aborted.

The adoption of certain observations regarding the use of words in the proclamation of the Word seems in order:

(1) Words determine whether or not the idea conceived is the idea communicated. The words chosen and the tonal quality may have

more influence on what is conveyed than the content of the Word of God itself. Spoken words are sound waves that strike the eardrums and are carried immediately to the brain centers. But what the brain receives is determined by many factors other than what is intended to be sent. George Eliot said it well: "Our words have wings, but fly not where we would."

(2) There are words that have emotional hooks and when they are used, the presence of the emotional hooks should be borne in mind. One who is pastor of a congregation will more than likely be aware of words that are particularly emotion-laden, although there is an occasional experience when this is not the case and the pastor offends or fails to communicate because of the words chosen. To preach before a congregation of different racial and cultural background from that to which the preacher is accustomed may well present some problems with regard to the use of words. For example, the word "conservative" used by a White preacher before a Black congregation is laden with emotion. That, prima facie, often means "enemy." Also, the word "Negro" or "Colored" may have negative impact. This may also be the case when the listening congregation represents an educational or socioeconomic level different from that to which the preacher is accustomed.

(3) There are colloquialisms in the use of words of which the preacher must be aware. A minister going into a new community or just visiting in one different from his or her own must put forth some effort to understand some of the colloquial expressions in order to minimize barriers to communication. It is well known that words used in a certain section of the country often have meanings quite different in another section.

(4) Words in the form of mere angry rhetoric or incendiary verbalization do not constitute social crisis preaching. Often this is simply a rhetorical channel for the exteriorization of feelings and, hence, insufficient for the proclamation of the Word of God. To be sure, there are some speakers who are quite adept at the use of angry rhetoric. It must be admitted that such speaking may at times achieve a positive good. Sometimes it conveys to a listener—or group of listeners—the fact that the matter at hand is one which is considered to be extremely serious by the speaker. There are times when incendi-

ary verbalization gains the attention that a calmer form of speech would fail to gain.

The point to be remembered is that mere incendiary rhetoric is not social crisis preaching. It is not the proclamation of the Word of God in critical times. Perhaps, at times, a bit of anger is essential in the proclamation of the Word. Jesus certainly practiced the morality of anger. But the anger expressed, however, must be related to the ends of the gospel itself.

(5) Words are a part of the design of the sermon and sometimes they set the very tone for the reception of the sermon. Martin Luther King, Jr. was one who understood the importance of his words for the design of the sermon. His words were never carelessly chosen and he never resorted to dull, unimaginative, prosaic language when more moving words were at hand. For example, in the sermon *Shattered Dreams*, he says, "To sink in the quicksands of fatalism is both intellectually and psychologically stifling."[2] The metaphors chosen communicate his point far better than prosaic language would. He could simply have said, "fatalism is undesirable." These less carefully chosen words would perhaps have communicated, but the tone of reception would have been different.

In addition to his fulfillment of his prophetic mission and the new heights to which he brought the movement for human rights, one ventures to say that a most vital factor in the immense popularity of Dr. King was his uncommon gift in the use of words.

(6) No matter how well chosen the words are, they still fail to convey the total message which is in the heart of the committed minister. Particularly is this true when he or she feels especially deeply about a particular crisis. Many a preacher, totally committed to the cause of human rights and seeing the struggle lose significant ground, understands and identifies with Abraham Cowley's reference to "words that weep and tears that speak." Remember the words of Alfred Lord Tennyson in *In Memoriam:*

> I sometimes hold it half a sin
> To put in words the grief I feel;

---

[2]Martin Luther King, *Strength to Love* (New York: Pocket Books, 1968) 99.

For words, like nature, half reveal
And half conceal the Soul within.

(7) The use of high-sounding words with which the congregation is not familiar accomplishes no good. There are some ministers who thoughtlessly use terms that communicate nothing to the congregation. Others do it "with malice aforethought." That is to say, they use unfamiliar terms because of the notion that they will be appreciated for their "much-speaking."

THE PERCEPTUAL POWER OF FOCUS

Social crisis preaching may actually aid the preacher in sharpening his or her tools. This process of developing content and structure in order to speak to a social crisis is often helpful to the preacher.

During the civil rights era of the sixties many communities held weekly mass meetings for the purpose of providing information on the progress of the "movement," for the recruitment of participants, for raising funds, and for providing inspiration and encouragement. Speakers on those occasions were usually ministers who rose to uncommon heights in the presentation of their mass meeting sermons. One could easily see that much of the power of their message was in the fact that they had specific focus as opposed to the vague, hit-and-miss preaching often done on Sunday mornings.

The social crisis preacher does not ignore other realities. Rather, he or she will have a sense of what is primary and what is secondary and will communicate to the congregation their relative places in the whole picture. The secondary is not, by that fact, superfluous; it is a part of the whole.

The preacher must take care not to fall into the trap of trying to decide whether the gospel or the social crisis is primary. In a sense, social crisis preaching may be seen as bifocal because both are primary here. In a more profound sense, however, these are one inasmuch as social crisis preaching is the proclamation of that which is crucially relevant within the context of the Christian gospel in times of social crisis.

STRUCTURE

To consider the issue of structure or form in relation to crisis preaching may well seem to be the epitome of folly. Preoccupation with form is considered by some to be useless and a waste of time. The question arises, how could one ever find time or inclination to do so in times of social upheaval or crisis? When the community is caught up in grave crises and preachers recognize their responsibility to speak out, would they not forfeit what they are trying to do if form becomes a factor in the preparation and presentation of their messages?

Perhaps it is basically important to realize that the preacher or any public speaker, for that matter, does not have the choice of having structure or not having it. Rather, his or her choice is between having either a "thought-out" structure or one that is not carefully "thought-out." It must be confessed that there are times when form is not carefully thought out and the sermon has great power. The point is that the chances of effectiveness in the presentation of an urgent message that addresses social crises are greatly reduced when no thought is given to the manner of presentation and when the preacher does not have the natural gifts to embark upon an effective form without deliberate effort.

Form is essential to existence, and this includes the existence of ideas. That which is considered to be an idea that does not have form is but a vague impression. So, when one preaches, whether thought is given to it or not, form is a factor in the presentation. Davis[3] calls attention to the fact that there are forms of order and there are forms of disorder.

Since such crucial matters are at stake in social crisis preaching, it becomes even more important that the preacher consider the value of effective form to avoid some of the aimless preaching of which so many are guilty. In some cases those who preach do so simply because at a certain hour on a certain day of the week they are expected to do something called preaching. Perhaps it does not matter whether

---

[3]H. Grady Davis, *Design for Preaching* (Philadelphia: Muhlenberg Press) 2, 3.

form is considered here or not. On the other hand, when the preacher is trying to deal with a crisis, it is important that his or her words find their mark.

Because neither life nor ideas are possible without form, the real task of the preacher becomes that of finding the form that already belongs to the idea of making it as effective as possible. Of course, this may mean different things to different people.

Both consciously and unconsciously people respond to form as well as content or substance. This is true of the highly emotional "folk" church where the preacher holds forth with great zeal, rhythm, and ecstasy and it is true of the sophisticated audiences whose preacher presents his or her measured words and reasoned conclusions with intellectual respectability. Both preachers give attention to form. The fiery proclaimer of the word may not employ form based upon speech and homiletics textbooks, but it is generally a carefully developed manner of presentation. Needless to say, the preacher with "intellectual respectability" gives thought to the order of his or her presentation. The extent and quality of the response in both instances is due in part to the form employed by the speaker.

It should be understood that the response is not always a reasoned one. Davis suggests: "Our response to form seems to take place at levels of awareness deeper than *rational* thought, and may never *rise* to conscious attention. It begins deep down among the intuitive feelings. A man or woman would have a hard time figuring out the reason why he/she likes the shape of a certain automobile. He or she either likes it or does not like it long before he/she knows why. The lines and proportions affect him, do something to him in a quite irrational way . . . However, the work of a designer of automobile bodies requires him to know exactly what he is doing, to study form and to master its use."[4] The same is true of the proclaimer of the gospel during social crisis.

Effective Crisis Preaching is Usually Form-Conscious. The most effective social crisis preaching is form-conscious and much of its effectiveness is dependent thereupon. Obviously, these preachers, *in the heat of the battle*, did no research on the form desirable. They either

---

[4]Ibid., 3.

had some natural gifts in that direction or they had prepared themselves in advance of the advent of the particular crisis.

The crisis preacher is a designer. Somewhere in his or her thinking there must be an awareness of how people respond to form, although this cannot be the preacher's preoccupation. He or she is concerned to be heard and that is the burden of what is being said here. It does not matter how good a case the preacher has or how urgent the matter is with which he or she is concerned; it has no meaning whatsoever if it does not get heard. There are numerous examples of the ability of crisis preachers in designing their messages.

The speaking of Martin Luther King, Jr. was quite form-conscious. The tremendous response he received, both in terms of immediate reaction and the more qualitative response, came not only because of his manner of presentation.

In his preaching King would build his case with well placed, picturesque words and graphic descriptions. Both theologically and methodologically he was deductive in his procedures. He ordered his thoughts according to a definite plan. The idea that he expressed at the end would never have been presented in that form in the beginning. His tone of voice and the development of the thought being presented usually conformed to a definite style and form.

Virtually all preachers and speakers who are able to hold an audience give considerable attention to form. They are always either very concerned about their manner of presentation or they have the natural gift to speak with appealing form without giving thought to it.

Jessie Jackson, head of PUSH, demonstrates social crisis preaching. His sermons are designed to achieve maximum response on the part of his hearers. Sometimes they aim at boycotting a given business. Jackson skillfully designs his message so that members of his audience will maintain their interest throughout. His sermons may be long, but they are designed to capture the attention of the listeners for the entire message. He has such a diverse audience that special attention must be given to the forcefulness with which he appeals to every segment of it. For the young he uses much of the language with which they are most familiar and with which they can identify; for the older Blacks who come from the South he shows a remarkable ability to employ some of the style of the old-time Black preacher; for those who are interested in his ideas alone, he shows a thorough grasp of contemporary issues and thought about them. He presents all three of these without apparent loss of any part of that varied audience at any point. Much of this is due to the skillful arrangement of the presentation of ideas and projects.

THE RELATIONSHIP OF STRUCTURE TO CONTENT

In order for the social crisis sermon to find its mark, it must exhibit a union of content and structure. While appropriate emphasis has been placed upon the importance of intentional form, it must be understood that form does not precede substance. Davis observed, "The right form derives from the substance of the message itself, is inseparable from the content, becomes one with the content, and gives a feeling of finality to the sermon."[5] The form that is most appropriate, then, is inherent in the idea. The preacher must not superimpose a structure upon a sermon when such structure does not fit the idea. The types of outlines for social crisis preaching, which will be suggested a bit later, must depend upon the specific content of the sermon.

The speaking of Martin Luther King, Jr. demonstrated the skillful blending of form, content, and delivery. The structure of his messages always fit the content. An example of this is his sermon, "Three Dimensions of a Complete Life," based on Revelation 21:16. Here he uses the traditional three points, but these are indicated in both the sermon title and the scripture text. The first point that he makes has to do with *length* of life. The second is the *breadth* of life and the third is *height*. The mere outline gives the feeling of movement; each point builds on the other until the ultimate is reached in the third and final point. Here is the feeling of finality to which Davis refers. Not only does the sermon depict the dimensions of a complete life; it also demonstrates the dimensions of a complete sermon.

Some crisis preaching is so effective that when the preacher reaches the end of his or her sermon the listeners are ready to do

---

[5]Ibid., 9.

something about the cause represented immediately. The same content can be less skillfully arranged and the people will hear it with a measure of detached appreciation.

"UNSTRUCTURED STRUCTURE" IN CRISIS PREACHING

Since there is no such thing as a sermon without structure and there are sermons that accomplish the desired ends without planned structure, these may, in paradoxical fashion, be said to have "unstructured structure." That is to say, it is structure that the speaker did not consciously prepare but appears at the appropriate time. There are a variety of times and situations when this is done with varying degrees of success.

For one thing, there are those especially talented persons who can simply embark upon the right structure without effort or forethought. Their message naturally "falls" together into a beautiful and graphic design. Here the preacher feels no need to structure his or her sermon consciously. Then there are those impromptu occasions when there is not time for thought to be given to formal preparation and something must be said immediately. The preacher may, in such situations, discover some latent ability in relation to the effective use of unstructured structure or, it must be faced, he or she may discover his or her inabilities in this area. The situation may be so emotionally charged that the preacher is not able to structure a message. The preacher may discover an ability that shows up in such cases of crisis.

While the primary concern is with the preacher's task as he or she appears before a congregation in a regular setting during times of crisis, the importance of gatherings formed around a specific crisis cannot be overlooked.

The civil rights mass meeting sermon was usually offered by someone with some organic and/or emotional tie with the prevailing crisis. He or she was one who could deal with the issues in a detached fashion. Also, he or she was usually one who did not feel the inclination to structure a message for the occasion.

Mass meeting preachers were often so effective in the presentation of properly proportioned form and content, coupled with ecstasy and obvious inspiration that one was exceedingly glad to be on the same side. They were usually neither written nor formally prepared. They exhibited unstructured structure at its best.

One main suggestion here is that the more involved one is in a crisis—in terms of remedial action—the more likely hidden abilities are to come to the surface and manifest themselves. Who can tell what God can and will do with one who is completely immersed in a righteous cause? This is the kind of situation in which the preacher can surprise himself or herself.

ORDER FOR STRUCTURED
CRISIS PROCLAMATION

It has been suggested that Martin Luther King, Jr. usually used the deductive order of proclamation. The deductive order (sometimes called *direct* or *didactic*) places the central idea and position of the speaker before the audience at the very outset. The remaining part of the sermon will be devoted to delineating, substantiating or explaining the position thus stated.

The thesis upon which the sermon is based is stated clearly and concisely at the very beginning and there is no question in the minds of the hearers to what that is. When the general setting is calm and the issue to be discussed is without serious or pronounced emotional hooks, the direct method may not present any problem whatsoever. In fact, some will be grateful for the minister's candor and directness. On the other hand, when the sermon is delivered during a time of serious crisis and it is clear that most members of the congregation will be emotionally attached to a position that is different from that which the preacher feels compelled to present, much courage and skill may be required to employ the deductive or direct method.

Once, when a tough decision had to be made in a congregation and it was known that to make the right decision would create strife, a deacon remarked, "well you can't shoot a gun easy!" The direct method of crisis proclamation entails such a position. It simply does not dally with life or death issues. This is often the mood of those who choose the deductive method.

The deductive or direct method of proclamation may take one of two forms. It may have a *miniature inductive* beginning or it may be *abruptly direct.* The *miniature inductive* beginning would take place during the introduction. In this instance the introduction softens the blow of the presentation of the major point. Some will find this type of introduction necessary even when they feel called upon to "tell it like it is" without evasion or delay. Here the introduction moves gently but positively on to the basic thesis of the sermon. It employs a brief indirect procedure to make a direct announcement of a position and call to action.

For example, if the sermon is to express opposition to war or to a specific war, the introduction may discuss the gospel's demand that clear positions be expressed on moral issues. War is always a grave matter and it requires the careful attention of those committed to the cause of Christ. It may not be until he or she has ended his or her carefully worked introduction that the preacher states what his or her position is in specific terms and what action the preacher is suggesting. This is a deductive or direct order, but it is preceded by a *miniature* inductive beginning.

There may be value in considering some of the reasons the crisis proclaimer of the Word will choose the direct method of proclamation. *The direct method may at times be chosen with the hope that the sheer forthrightness and honesty of the preacher will aid in getting reception for his or her crisis proclamation.* Sometimes the preacher will know the hearers are in no mood to be toyed with when they are confronted with burning issues and will feel an honest statement must be made with regard to those issues. Such ministers know people are likely to appreciate their not playing games with them, but proceeding with what must be said. While that does not always mean they will accept the preacher's point of view, it may mean they will respect it and the preacher, which in turn may help in gaining acceptance of that point of view.

When a social crisis exists the parishioners and persons of the community will usually be aware of it and, if the preacher has been consistent in his/her social concerns, they will know generally what his/her position will be. Thus, a direct statement is in order. No purpose would be served by delaying the impact of the position of the preacher on the issue. Both supporters of the position that the preacher is expected to take and opponents of that position will be waiting for him/her to expand upon that point of view. The preacher then has upon that point the opportunity to increase support for his or her position or, of course, to lose support. That possibility must not be taken lightly. At any rate, nothing will be accomplished by delay.

The abruptly direct order may be chosen for its shock value. There are times when the congregation will simply need to be shocked into the realization of the gravity of an existing situation. They may know that it exists, but have no perception of the relevance of the grave situation for themselves. A suburban congregation is not likely to feel particularly involved in a problem that may exist in the central city, even though they may have a *casual* relationship to that problem. The social crisis preacher may have the responsibility of informing the members that they are, indeed, involved and that to delay dealing with a problem is not to avoid it. It may take a shock to secure their undivided attention.

In such an instance no miniature inductive procedure will be employed. There will be no delay in coming to the point. Immediately and forthrightly, the preacher comes forth with the statement of a position that he or she knows will be controversial and may lose friends or even church members. The very first words of the preacher may be diametrically opposed to what the church or the community consider to be valid or "wise."

The preacher understands that this procedure may well be a declaration of war, but he or she will know that for a ministry to be productive and honest, it will not be a succession of Palm Sundays and Easters without the accompanying Good Fridays. Clearly, this procedure may well evoke immediate hostility and may even erect a barrier to further communication at the moment. Upon hearing the initial statement they may deliberately choose not to listen further.

Sometimes such a procedure will command attention as nothing else could do, and members of the listening congregation dare not allow their minds to wander. It then is the preacher's responsibility to use the attention gained and to win friends and supporters for the cause espoused. If the preacher is confident and courageous, as well as skillful, he or she may receive a positive response.

Stating a boldly controversial position in an abrupt manner may cause some to raise very pointed questions with the preacher; this should be desirable for it affords him or her the opportunity to deal with the particular crisis with the people on a one-to-one basis.

So courage is required in employing this method of presenting a point of view with regard to a social crisis. The preacher who feels the mantle of Jesus Christ and that of the ancient prophets upon his/her shoulders will not shy away from the dangers inherent in taking a bold stand.

Many persons, for various reasons, will deal with social issues from an unpopular perspective by using the *indirect* method. This is sometimes called the *inductive* procedure. This procedure is the opposite of the direct method. Here the preacher will work into the major thesis of the sermon. He or she will either use a relevant illustration or other device to get started, but the congregation will not be told immediately what the minister is really getting across.

The preacher whose congregation is conservative but who is genuinely interested in presenting a point of view contrary to the canons of conservatism will find this procedure particularly useful.

THE SOCIAL CRISIS SERMON OUTLINE

Some popular preachers refuse to use the outline method of sermon development. In order for the sermon to have organization and to be remembered by the hearers, this method is quite valid if not imperative.

While any effective type of sermon outline is useful for social crisis preaching, there are some that seem to lend themselves to this kind of proclamation in a special way.

The interrogative outline. Since much of social crisis preaching will be controversial and many questions are likely to be asked about the particular issue, the interrogative outline may be useful. Each point or section of the sermon may be introduced with a pertinent question regarding the issue. These may well be questions that the preacher knows to be on the minds of members of the congregation. Also, it should be acknowledged that the preacher does not have all of the answers all of the time, nor should he or she be expected to have them. Therefore, it may be legitimate to raise questions in the sermon that will be addressed but perhaps not answered. They could be questions on which preacher and people must work together in order to find answers.

The problem solving outline. In this instance the problem will be some matter in which the community has a special stake. A problem exists in the community. The outline would include: statement of the problem itself; statement of the Biblical principle that is applicable; strategies and techniques that can be applied; the plan and program for solution. The problem solving outline may also involve the motivated sequence in which members of the congregation progress along with the preacher in pursuit of a solution to a given problem. In such case, the sermon may begin with the problem and the Biblical principle together. As the sermon proceeds, each point will lead into another similar to what Ilion T. Jones calls the "Ladder" or "Unfolding Telescope" outline. The end will be a probable solution to the problem.

The Hegelian or Triadic Outline. This form is based on what is called in some quarters the Hegelian scheme. It is based upon the philosophy of Georg Wilhelm Friedrich Hegel who developed a notion of the conflict of opposites that could be resolved only with the recognition of their interdependence. Contradictory realities imply and require each other, according to this perspective as is evident in Hegel's *Philosophy of History* and his *Philosophy of Right*, which include the thesis, the antithesis, and the synthesis. The thesis is the expression of one reality while the antithesis is the opposing reality. For Hegel, these are reconciled in the synthesis in which they are actually united.

In social crisis preaching, there are conflicting ideas. The preacher's sermon may state at the outset his or her *thesis*, which is the statement of a proposition. The second point would be the antithesis, which argues with the first point. These two are combined to form the synthesis.

Example: "Human Crisis and God's Timetable"
Text: Mark 1:14-15

(Introduction)

Thesis: God has a timetable for the resolution of human crises ("The time is fulfilled. . . .")

Antithesis: Crises are abated by human effort ("John . . . appeared in the wilderness, preaching [v. 4] . . . was arrested . . . Jesus came . . . preaching. . . .")

Synthesis: God's timetable is revealed by the combination of human effort and belief and divine involvement.

DELIVERY OF THE SOCIAL CRISIS SERMON

There is no need for extensive treatment of the issue of the delivery of social crisis sermons in the present work. Sound principles for the delivery of sermons of any sort would generally apply here. A few suggestions, however, may be useful:

(1) Social crisis sermons may be delivered with or without manuscript or notes. The capacity of the individual preacher may determine which will be employed. The preacher who does not use notes needs to take care lest the sermon be without effective organization and, indeed, may be without the desired and intended content. Many who preach without manuscript or notes prepare notes in advance but simply do not use them in delivery. Others organize their sermons in their minds and present them with no visible notes to refer to. Among the effective preachers who preached without notes in the presentation of social crisis sermons were Martin Luther King, Jr., Mordecai Wyatt Johnson, and Howard Thurman.

The use of manuscript has had a varied history. Its use has ranged all the way from the report of a minister having been driven from his pulpit for raising his eyes from his manuscript during the reign of Henry VIII to the decree issued by the General Assembly of the Church of Scotland, which declared that reading sermons was "displeasing to God's people."[6] The user of a manuscript should not allow this process to diminish the forthrightness or force of the social crisis sermon. Also, maintaining eye contact is particularly important in this kind of preaching.

(2) Since social crisis preaching is often done in times of heightened emotions and pronounced tensions, the preacher must strive to

---

[6]As reported in Ilion T. Jones, *Principles and Practice of Preaching* (Nashville TN: Abingdon Press, 1957) 189.

maintain control in sermon delivery while not removing nor diminishing the emotional element. Some preachers have been known to completely lose control of themselves during the presentation of a crisis-conscious message and thus fail to communicate what was intended. The fire and passion must not be removed but some measure of control must be maintained.

(3) The particular style of delivery should be determined by the personality and natural equipment of the preacher. Some will discover that a conversational style of delivery is best suited for them and for the people they serve. Others will find a more formal style of delivery more effective for them. Black preachers often employ what has been called "the aesthetic of sound" in crisis and other presentation. (Of course, it must be recalled that there is no monolithic Black preacher nor Black preaching style, although some styles dominate.)

(4) Getting across a social crisis sermon will be aided by the employment of variety in pitch and force on the part of the preacher.

(5) Diaphragmatic breathing, clarity of enunciation, and projection of the voice will be most helpful in communicating the social crisis sermon.

THE "POST-DELIVERY" FUNCTION OF THE PREACHER

St. Augustine's words, "If a man's life be lightning his words are thunder," are applicable to the social crisis preacher in a special way. The suggestion is that words and life are part of the same process and are therefore inseparable. Social crisis proclamation, like any other preaching, must be continuous with the "pre-delivery" and "post-delivery" function of the preacher. The thunder and the lightning go together.

The vast amount of literature produced in the field of preaching gives attention to both the mechanics of preaching and to the preacher himself or herself. Unfortunately, however, the scales are tipped in the direction of the mechanics while scant attention is given to the life and commitment of the preacher. Far more attention is devoted to what the preacher must do than to who the preacher must be.

A number of the Lyman Beecher lecturers devoted their entire lecture series to the person who preaches; others have included this emphasis in their work. William Jewett Tucker, who spoke on "The Making and the Unmaking of the Preacher," made the comment, "Great truths announce their presence before they are formulated."[7] To that may be added the fact that great truths continue their presence after they are formulated and proclaimed. This continuation is effected through the members of the congregation and the minister in their living. In the very last paragraph of his homiletics classic, John A. Broadous calls attention to the power of character and life to reinforce speech. "What a preacher is goes far to determine the effect of what he says."[8]

Effective social crisis preaching requires life commitment to the cause of justice and liberation. No matter how endowed the preacher is with natural gifts, knowledge, and skill, the proclamation will be anemic and ultimately ineffectual when the preacher is simply delivering a message. Something of one's commitment expresses itself in the force and power of the social crisis sermon. Howard Thurman, in *Disciplines of the Spirit*, says that commitment is the yielding of the nerve center to consent to that which is more than life itself. Those whose daily lives are lived in the fear and admonition of the God who has a special concern for the oppressed will reveal this commitment in their proclamation. There must be personal involvement and action before and after the sermon is presented. The function of the sermon is not completed when the final point is made. This is especially true of social crisis preaching.

In more specific terms, the question may be raised as to what the preacher with social sensitivity must do. Simply put, he or she must believe and act on the Word of God. This observation is not as far-fetched and divorced from reality as some might suppose. Those whose profession, whose *job* it is to preach may well see it simply as a job or as a profession with no particular application to themselves. Not only does the Word of God apply *also* to the preacher; it applies to him or her with intimidating impact and special meaning. Some-

---

[7]As quoted in Edgar DeWitt Jones, *The Royalty of the Pulpit* (New York: Harper & Brothers Publishers, 1951) 189.

[8]John A. Broadous, *On The Preparation and Delivery of Sermons* (New York: Harper & Row Brothers, 1944) 377.

one has put it this way: The minister ought not to be any better than other people ought to be, but the minister must be better than other people *are*. The Word of God applies to the proclaimer of that Word with peculiar force. Even with adherence to this mandate, the preacher can assume no status of special species, for it is still a treasure contained in fragile earthen vessels.

Hear the conclusion of the whole matter: Believe and act on the powerful and uncompromising Word of Almighty God.

APPENDIX A
TRUTH-POWER
AND LOVE-POWER
IN A COURT
OF TESTIMONY
CHOANG-SENG SONG*

But before all this happens they will set upon you and persecute you. You will be brought before synagogues and put in prison; you will be haled before kings and governors for your allegiance to me. This will be a time for you to bear testimony; so make up your minds not to prepare your defense beforehand, because I myself will give you a mouth (power of utterance) and a wisdom which no opponent will be able to resist or refute.

LUKE 21:12-15[1]

---

*In Justo L. González, *Proclaiming the Acceptable Year* (Valley Forge PA: Judson Press, 1982) 27-39.

[1]The passage used here combines the renderings in the Revised Standard Version (RSV) and the New English Bible (NEB).

STRANGE ADVICE

What strange advice Jesus has given to his disciples: Do not prepare your defense before kings and governors! This is not the only time that Jesus gives such strange advice. He seems to do it constantly. It almost looks as if he has made it a principle not to give any advice that is not out of the ordinary.

"Do not be anxious about tomorrow," Jesus once told a big crowd of people, "tomorrow will look after itself. Each day has troubles enough of its own" (Matthew 6:34, NEB). Overworked laborers, worried farmers, and tired mothers in the crowd must have nodded and said, "Amen," to his last few words. "Each day has troubles enough of its own." This is the fact of life, is it not? Look at those weary faces in the streets and in crowded buses and subway trains! They bear marks of cares and struggles people go through in life, not only each day, but each week, each month, and each year. Because each day has troubles enough of its own, we must brace ourselves for tomorrow, for next week, for next month, and even for next year. This is our logic. We cannot let tomorrow take care of itself. To avoid disaster, we must take care of tomorrow. But Jesus has an entirely different logic. For him tomorrow will take care of itself. But how?

I find this logic of Jesus at once fascinating and disturbing. It throws off balance our conventions, which have grown sterile and oppressive. We wish to applaud him for his bold logic, but we are also worried and feel unsure.

Here is another typical example. Jesus was talking about friendship, hospitality, and social etiquette and out came this most unusual advice. "When you are having a party for lunch or supper," he said calmly, "do not invite your friends, your brothers or other relations, or your rich neighbors. . . . But when you give a party, ask the poor, the crippled, the lame, and the blind . . ." (Luke 14:12-14, NEB).

Is Jesus quite in his right mind? We wonder. Is a party still a party if it is not for friends and relatives? We carefully choose our guests for a dinner party. We make sure like-minded people are invited. We want to have a pleasant evening savored with witty remarks and enlivened with interesting conversations. We also want to renew and cultivate our social ties. This is what a party is for. As to the poor, the lame, and the blind, we have a lot going for them. The church runs special projects—orphanages, poor people's homes, clinics, and rehabilitation centers. But Jesus does not seem very much impressed. He insists on talking about a party, not projects, for the marginalized people.

Well, is Jesus not going too far in this instance? Yes, he does go very far. Yet, in fact, he always gives us the impression that he has not gone far enough. He exasperates us. He makes us wonder. But we have to admit one thing: Jesus' whole life was a party for the poor, the blind, the oppressed, and the outcast. He held his party for them in all sorts of imaginable places—in open fields, at street corners, by roadsides. Jesus drank and ate with them. He listened to their complaints and shared their agonies. He healed them and gave them power to hope. It was a long painful party mingled with innocent laughter, thankful tears, and deep sighs. Most dramatic of all, that party did not end in a palace where Jesus might have been crowned as king; it ended on a cross where he was put to death as a political agitator.

What a strange life! And what a strange party! There is something powerful in that life. There is something inviting in that party. What is it? It is the power that liberates people from themselves and from their weaknesses. It is the faith that makes God's presence in the world real. It is the love that joins God and people in struggle for the kingdom of God on earth. The cross is this power, this faith, and this love. Because of that cross, Jesus gives strange advice not to worry about tomorrow and not to hold a party just for friends and relatives, especially not for rich neighbors. And above all, in the name of that cross, he bids us stand before kings and rulers totally unprepared for our own defense.

CHRISTIANS IN A COURTROOM

The court is the scene of activities here. Seated high on the pedestal are judges who represent the power and authority of the state. As individual persons, they are not different from any other people, not even from the defendants standing before them. They have their private desires and secret ambitions as you and I do. They have to worry about tomorrow as we do. Just as the defendants before them, they have family and social obligations to fulfill. Enclosed in those menacing black robes are ordinary human beings: weak, vulnerable, and corruptible. But when they put on state authority, they become transformed. They have the power to condemn or to forgive. They have the authority to imprison or to set free. This is, in fact, what Pontius Pilate, the Roman governor, told Jesus: "Surely you know that I have authority to release you, and I have authority to crucify you?" (John 19:10, NEB).

"I will give you a mouth," says Jesus to Christians in court. But judges, too, have a mouth. Of course they have a mouth, a big, big, powerful mouth! The mouth they have in the martial law court is not the mouth ordinary citizens use to speak with, to eat with, to laugh with, to sigh with, or to joke with. It is a mouth given to them by the state with a tremendous power of utterance. It speaks for kings and presidents. It announces the decrees of a military regime. It declares the mind of an authoritarian ruler. And all this with a solemn air of legality and constitutionality! That mouth quotes the law right and left. It recites the litany of freedom of the press, of speech, of religion, and of conscience stipulated in the Constitution. It praises the enforcement of law and order that makes that precious freedom possible. And yet at the end of the long demanding day, out from that powerful state mouth comes a most dreaded utterance: Guilty! That mouth does not pronounce the verdict halfheartedly. It does it with a tone of finality. You are guilty! You are an enemy of the state! The case is closed. Further appeal is just a matter of formality.

It is to such a state court that some Christians are brought today in Asia and elsewhere. What have they done? What crime have they committed? Until very recently, Christians in Asia have been law-abiding citizens; most of them still are. But some have been accused of breaking the law of the state. They have been arrested by the police, tried before the military court, and declared guilty of attempted overthrow of the government. But all they have done is urge their government to observe human rights. They have affirmed that democracy and not dictatorship is what people desire. They have pointed out social and political evils that in the end would plunge the nation into chaos.

In 1974 the Council of Bishops of the Roman Catholic Church in South Korea pledged to do its utmost "to recover the original sanctity of all (people) in Christ, to break down the barriers of human discrimination, falsehood, and mistrust, that all may enjoy love and peace as brothers and sisters."[2] Is this not a noble ideal that should appeal not only to Christians but also to all citizens? Who has no need for sanctity to live as human beings? Who wants to remain a victim of discrimination, falsehood, and mistrust? And who will not enjoy love and peace? But those in power read this noble ideal differently. They saw in it a challenge to their power. They took it as posing a question to their authority, and they decided to silence the voice of Christian conscience.

This has become a familiar story repeated over and over again in many countries in Asia in recent years. Out of their faith in Jesus Christ, Christians feel compelled to speak the truth. But truth is the number one enemy of those who rule with military and police power. They are not content with a monopoly of power; they want to have a monopoly of truth as well. There is no truth but their truth. There is no power but their power. They pronounce guilty those Christians who honestly question the rulers' truth and sincerely request the rulers to curb their power. Truth must serve power. If truth refuses, it

---

[2]T. K., *Letters from South Korea*, ed. Sekai and trans. David L. Swain (New York: IDOC/North America, Inc., 1976) 216.

must be arrested, tried, and put behind bars. It is power that judges, not truth. It is guns that have the final word, not conscience, even if it is a Christian conscience. This is the way it is in South Korea, in Taiwan, in the Philippines, and in many other countries in the world today.

Listen to these words that concluded an eyewitness account of the bloody suppression of Thai student riots in Bangkok in October, 1973; they were protesting against their corrupt and inept government.

> I saw mobs of people.
> I saw mobs of beasts.
> . . . the Thai people remain in a state of slavery.
> They are the tools of those who want to achieve more power,
> and of those who are afraid of losing their power.
> They are pawns that can be manipulated
> and experimented upon by different ideologies. . . .
> The pattern is clear,
> the pattern woven by the mighty and powerful,
> the power lies at the end of the gun
> or in brutal force.[3]

Power is all that counts. Power to the rulers! Then people can talk about democracy. Only then can people toy with freedom. Democracy and freedom at the point of the gun!

The court is a formidable instrument of the state power that has made itself judge of all people and all things. It is before such a court that Christians stand accused of a grave crime against the state. The state prosecutor has the prosecution against them ready. Fully armed military police stand at attention behind them. There is no escape from the all-powerful state.

Yet these Christians still have something free—their mouths! Their mouths are not incarcerated. They still have some power of utterance. This is the time to open their mouths. In their own defense they can still say something. They must defend their innocence. They can declare how much they love the nation and its people, appeal to the conscience of their rulers, and stress that they are moti-

---

[3]See *Testimony Amidst Asian Suffering*, ed. T. K. Thomas (Singapore: Christian Conference of Asia, 1977) 13.

vated by a vision of a free and democratic society. Their zeal, their
sincerity, and their eloquence may still move the judges and soften
their hearts.

To speak in one's own defense in court is a most natural thing. It
is a must. Too much is at stake here to keep one's mouth shut. Loss of
physical freedom is a real possibility. Bleak lonely years of prison life
are ahead. That is why defendants must speak out. They must hire
defense lawyers to speak for them. This is the time they must put their
mouths to full use. They must muster power of utterance at this critical moment.

MAKE NO PREPARATION FOR YOUR DEFENSE

Jesus advises his followers to the contrary, "Make no preparation
for your defense." This advice contradicts common practice. It offends common sense. Jesus should have advised Christians to open
their mouths in defense against state prosecution. He should have
urged them to hire lawyers—the more experienced the lawyers are,
the better—to speak on their behalf. But, no! "Make up your minds,"
he tells them, "not to prepare your defense beforehand." Brought to
trial in a military court with no preparation for defense? Why should
Christians be different from other defendants? Why must they alone
submit to the whims and complicities of state power?

I am sure such questions at once come up in your mind. You must
be puzzled. I am puzzled, too. How could one take such advice seriously? It just would not work. It would only make Christians play into
the hands of state authorities. Their silence would only confirm that
the state is right. The mass media under state control would report
that the defendants admitted their crime by their silence. Silence is
no virtue at a military court. Absolutely not!

"Make no preparation for your defense in advance." We may not
like the advice, even if it is from Jesus. We may be offended by it; but
still, it is there. It will not disappear from our Bible. What are we then
to make of it? Coming from Jesus, it must have some deep truth in it.
What could that truth be? How are we to grasp it?

I must at this point draw your attention to the reason that
prompted Jesus to give that strange advice. Most pointedly he tells us
why you wind up in court, of all places, to begin with. "You will be

haled before kings and governors," he says, "for your allegiance to me." Yes, here is the clue. You are brought to trial not because you have been engaged in a business fraud, not because you robbed a bank or committed a murder. You are there in court for your allegiance to Jesus. Your faith in Jesus has gotten you into trouble with state power. It is all because of Jesus. This at once makes you different from other defendants. Because of Jesus, you have said that political oppression must stop. Because of him, you demanded a social and political reform that is motivated by the welfare of all people and not by the interest of those in power. True to your commitment to him, you made it known that exploitation of people by an authoritarian government works against God's will.

This is why you find yourself in a military court. You were not after political power; the secret police who arrested you know that. You did not try to form an opposition political party; the prosecutor who conducted the interrogation is aware of that. And the authorities do not believe you have the power to overthrow the government. The state power is not reckoning with your political power. You do not have political power. The church has little to do with political power. In most countries in Asia, Christians are small in number; therefore, how can they pit themselves against the powerful political machine of the ruling party?

The state does not have to worry about your political power. But there is one thing the state must worry about: the moral power that comes from your faith in Jesus. That they have to reckon with. It is as formidable as, if not more formidable than, state power. It speaks the truth and not lies. It does not call evil good and good evil. It echoes the agonies of men and women under the heavy burden of life. And above all, it calls for people to have a greater share in political decisions that affect their lives and future.

It is now time for the government and the church, the rulers and Christians, the brutal power of the state and the moral power of the faith to do battle. This is what happened in Taiwan, that small island in Asia ruled by the authoritarian Nationalist government with martial law for more than thirty years. In December, 1971, the Presbyterian Church in Taiwan broke its silence and spoke out:

The Executive Committee of the Presbyterian Church in Taiwan, which speaks for 200,000 Christians in Taiwan, wishes to express its extreme concern over developments in the world which could seriously affect the lives of all who live on this island. Based on our belief that Jesus Christ is the Lord of all people, the righteous judge and saviour of the world, we voice our concern and our request, and in doing so, we are convinced that we speak not only for the church but for all our compatriots.[4]

They were speaking in the name of Jesus for the entire population of the nation! It is a big claim for a small church to make. The government judged such a claim to be presumptuous, dangerous, and seditious, and a few years later, when the church's claim grew into a call for political reforms that would make Taiwan into a free and independent nation, the government decided that it had had enough. It put the church's leaders on trial, charging that they aided in acts of sedition against the state.

Jesus is dead right. It is no ordinary trial that takes place in court. Christians who speak and act in allegiance to Jesus and who stand their trial in court have nothing to say in their defense. They have not broken the law, committed a crime, or attempted a sedition. This is all as clear as day. The prosecutor knows it and judges know it. Still the trial must be staged. Who then stands trial there? Who is called to account before the public? Not the Christians accused of sedition, but the state proceeding with its prosecution! Indicted in the military court are not Christians but the ruling power that makes the indictment. The long prosecution read out by the chief prosecutor is the self-prosecution of the government. The verdict pronounced by the presiding judge is a verdict on the military regime and not on the church. By bringing Christians to trial, those in power pronounce themselves guilty.

The strange advice of Jesus is not strange anymore. He himself acted on his own advice. When brought to Pontius Pilate for trial, he did not say anything in his own defense. For the first time in his career, Pilate was faced with a prisoner who refused to defend himself against accusations brought against him. Confronted with Jesus' stubborn silence, Pilate must have been puzzled, annoyed, and

---

[4]From "Public Statement on National Fate" issued by the Presbyterian Church in Taiwan on 30 December 1971.

frightened. He was overcome with the powerful presence of one he
had to condemn to death.

FROM A TRIAL COURT
TO A TESTIMONY COURT

I find this a most astonishing thing—that Christians are not to
prepare a defense. Yet in Jesus' advice there is something more astonishing, for he goes on to say: "This will be a time for you to bear
testimony." Do you see the dramatic change that has taken place
here? Do you perceive a momentous transformation of all that has to
do with the trial? Radically affected is the court itself. Christians
brought to trial because of their allegiance to Jesus have changed a
military court into a court of testimony! From a trial court to a testimony court! It is now a different court altogether. A completely new
situation has developed before our eyes. Proceedings of the trial have
now come to a temporary stop. The court is no longer the space and
time in which martial law reigns supreme. Right there, despite the
massive concentration of state power, martial law is suspended. The
testimony court called into being through the presence of Christian
defendants has created a new space and a new time in which a new
law takes command—the law of love!

What can be more astonishing than this! Jesus' strange advice has
proven to be a most powerful thing. The monster called emergency
rule and martial law has devoured many lives and cost many people
their freedom. It has turned the whole country into a prison house
and the people into prisoners. But now in the courtroom, a heavily
guarded territory of the monster, a small space of freedom for the
human spirit has been broached. It is not anymore a time of trial, but
a time of testimony. This free time and this free space, created by a
Christian presence in the courtroom, will eventually become people's space. A free zone is built within the unfree compound.

The judges sitting there in judgment and the prosecutors with
their written prosecution are taken by surprise. Like Pilate in ancient
times, they are puzzled and irritated, but at the bottom of their hearts
a little frightened and somewhat moved. For a few short moments
when the testimony of Christians fills the courtroom, the judges and
prosecutors become an audience to a strange testimony of Jesus' love

for people in suffering and in pain, people oppressed by unjust social and political power, and people uncertain about their future. For these few brief moments, they must feel indicted and judged. And again, just as Pilate, they must conclude that the Christians before them are innocent of the crime with which they have been charged. The judges perhaps want very much to free them, if only to ease their own conscience, but like Pilate, they are not free under the burden of state authority. For these few fleeting moments they must envy the freedom of those Christians in front of them, bearing testimony not to their innocence but to what God has done for humanity. And we do hear of small miracles that have happened in one of those testimony courts. The military prosecutor, at the conclusion of the trial of political dissidents in Taiwan in the spring of 1980, was moved to make just a small remark: the prosecution was military police, brought to the court to give false witness, kept silent and did not answer the presiding judge's questions.

"You will be haled before kings and governors for your allegiance to me," says Jesus. "This will be a time for you to bear testimony." For many Christians in Asia and elsewhere today, these words of Jesus have come true. How can it be otherwise? Just recall these lines in Mary's Magnificat, a most fitting prelude to the birth of an extraordinary child:

> The arrogant of heart and mind he has put to rout,
> he has brought down monarchs from their thrones,
>   but the humble have been lifted high.
> The hungry he has satisfied with good things,
>   the rich sent empty away.
>
> —Luke 1:51b-53, NEB

With the birth of the Savior Son, God intensified his revolution within the world. And what a revolution! It strives to liberate the poor from their poverty and the rich from their riches. It struggles to liberate the powerless from their powerlessness and the powerful from their power. It is a revolution that liberates the truth from lies that corrupt human hearts and pollute human community. In a court of testimony in the midst of a martial law courtroom, one catches a glimpse of such liberation.

It is a small revolution, but we begin to notice some changes. Of course the state continues to shout lies disguised as truths, but the people begin to whisper truths. The ruling power still loudly affirms its illegitimacy in the name of legitimacy, but the people start to make their legitimate claims that have, in this climate, the appearance of illegitimacy. The martial law regime continues to deny political freedom to the people on the pretext of national security, but the people are learning that, if there is no freedom and democracy, there will be no national security. Such small changes are taking place in people's hearts, in their homes behind closed doors, in the street corners sheltered from the vigilant eyes of the security police. As time goes on, people's whispers will grow louder and louder until the moment of truth arrives—the moment in which the power of the rulers has to take into account the power of the people. All this has a small beginning in a military court turned into a testimony court.

"Make up your minds not to prepare your defense beforehand." We can now better see why this has to be Jesus' advice. But Jesus does not end his advice there. It is already formidable advice, as we have seen, but there is something more to come from him. He goes on to tell us: "I myself will give you a mouth (power of utterance)!" That is it. This is the whole secret. Jesus himself will give us a mouth equipped with power of utterance. No wonder he asks us not to prepare our defense in advance.

"I myself will give you a mouth," says Jesus. The mouth we open in court is Jesus' mouth. The mouth with which we bear testimony is his mouth. The mouth from which words of love come is his mouth also. That is why Christians quote Jesus' words in reply to the judges' questions.

Several Christians, among them the general secretary of the Presbyterian Church in Taiwan were brought before a military court and tried for giving shelter to a political dissident hunted by the police in the aftermath of a human rights rally in Taiwan in December, 1979, that had turned into a riot. They testified in the words of Jesus: "Come to me, all who labour and are heavy laden, and I will give you rest. Take my yoke upon you, and learn from me; for I am gentle and lowly in heart, and you will find rest for your souls. For my yoke is easy, and my burden is light" (Matthew 11:28-30). And again:

"There is no greater love than this, that a man should lay down his life for his friends" (John 15:13, NEB).

On account of these words of our Lord Jesus, they said, we could not turn in to the authorities a man desperately seeking help. These words of Jesus must have sounded odd to some in the courtroom. Some must have derided them as out of place in a trial. But there must have been others who were moved by the power of love contained in them. The mouth of Jesus had spoken, and a powerful testimony to the God of love was made.

"I myself will give you power of utterance," promises Jesus. Left to fend for ourselves alone in court, what power of utterance can we still have? The utterance of the state court is so powerful that it reduces our defense to a plea for mercy. The speech of the prosecutor is delivered with such sonority that a defendant's words are rendered into a broken chord. And the presiding judge asks questions in such an overbearing manner that we feel confused and intimidated. But Jesus speaks of the power of utterance. Yes, he too speaks about power. He has not renounced power. What kind of power does he say he will give to us? It is the power of truth. It is the power of love. What Jesus gives is truth-power and love-power. It is this kind of power that he promised to give us in court. When that truth-power takes form in utterance-power, people hear what they have always wanted to hear—truth about the state of the nation. When that love-power is expressed in speech-power, people can distinguish black from white, right from wrong, and good from evil. What a power this is! Before this power of utterance the state power acting against people's conscience becomes a mere sounding gong and a clanging cymbal.

One of those Asian Christians who has demonstrated this remarkable power of utterance is Kim Chi Ha, a Korean Roman Catholic poet serving a life sentence in Seoul for his fight for freedom and democracy under a most authoritarian government. During the court interrogation in June, 1976, the chief prosecutor asked him: "As a writer and a poet, what are your views concerning freedom of expression?"

This was his reply: "Freedom of expression means freedom of speech or words. This is a basic tenet of democracy. The history of democracy is a history of the struggle for freedom of expression."[5] Silence that is choking people must be broken. "The culture of silence"[6] imposed by those in power to cover the truth from the eyes of the people must be exposed. Kim Chi Ha went on to testify: "Silence and speech are in opposition. Speech is that which rescues the truth from darkness. But silence is the evil power that throws the truth into darkness. The expression, 'the Word of God,' means that God himself is speech."[7] With such words Kim Chi Ha came so near to the heart of the Christian faith, the Word of God.

God himself has broken silence! This is what creation is about. Our God is not a talkative God. He does not bore us to death with clichés, slogans, and pep talks. But when chaos is on the rampage, when darkness threatens, then God speaks. And what a tremendous power of utterance he has! When he speaks, light appears and darkness is dispersed. When he opens his mouth, order returns to the universe. And when he utters his powerful words, life comes into being. Yes, God is Word. God is Speech. His Word is Power. His Speech is Life.

And this God has spoken in Jesus! Jesus is God's Word. He is God's Speech. That is why he "taught . . . as one who had authority, and not as the scribes" (Mark 1:22). His authority is God's authority. His power is God's power. Of course people were astonished. These learned doctors of the law, these meticulously pious leaders obsessed with traditions, talked a lot. But their words did not carry God's authority. There was no God's power in their speech. But when Jesus spoke, the blind received their sight, the dumb had their power of speech restored to them. When he spoke, those tormented in mind and in spirit found joy and hope. And when he spoke those most powerful words with his feeble voice in his last hour on the cross, "Father, forgive them . . ." (Luke 23:34), the Roman soldier at the scene of the

---

[5]Kim Chi Ha, *The Gold-Crowned Jesus and Other Writings*, ed. Chong Sun Kim and Shelly Killen (Maryknoll NY: Orbis Books, 1978) 59.

[6]Ibid., 59. Kim Chi Ha writes, "The 'culture of silence,' a term used in the Third World, refers to the gloomy conditions whereby those in power—the dictators, exploiters, and oppressors—cover the truth from the eyes of the people and paralyze any human thought or judgment."

[7]Ibid., 59.

crucifixion burst out: "Truly this man was the Son of God!" (Mark 15:39).

Kim Chi Ha was right. God is Speech. It is this God who gives power of utterance to the Christians who bear testimony in court. Their testimony joins the chorus of testimonies of Christians in the past. It will inspire future Christians to add their testimonies to the chorus. This mighty chorus of Christian testimonies will continue to be heard at the very seat of state authorities, to reverberate in people's hearts, and find echoes in the whole universe until the time when God will have made "all things new" (See Revelation 21:5). But in the meantime, a liberation of a most radical kind has taken place: most unfree Christians have become most free! For we know Jesus stands at our side in court with His quiet but firm voice: "This is a time for you to bear testimony. . . . I myself will give you power of utterance . . . which no opponent will be able to resist or refute." This is not strange advice anymore. It is a powerful promise and assurance.

APPENDIX B
BLACKNESS AS SIGN
AND ASSIGNMENT
GAYRAUD S. WILMORE*

> *Son of man, you dwell in the midst of a rebellious house*
> *. . . . Therefore, . . . prepare for yourself an exile's bag-*
> *gage, . . . for I have made you a sign for the house of*
> *Israel.*
>
> EZEKIEL 12:2-3, 6

*In Robert T. Newbold, ed., *Black Preaching* (Philadelphia: The Geneva Press, 1977) 165-73.

Many people are confused about blackness. The term is used in many different ways today and the result is thorough confusion. Black power, Black pride, Black studies, Black theology—what are we to make of blackness? Is the word nothing more than a kind of arbitrary synonym for Negro, colored, or Afro-American—or is there a more substantive meaning related to something eminently significant about us as a people? Let me put it another way: Is there a profound religious meaning in the idea of being a Black people?

Let me put it squarely before you. I believe Black Christians—the Black church in Africa and America—should articulate the theological meaning of blackness that arises from our religious experience as a people. I believe that we need to understand blackness as both a sign and an assignment from God.

Ezekiel is given a sign and an assignment from God. He had no choice in the matter. God didn't ask him if he would like to take on this assignment. He simply said: "Son of man, I have made you a watchman over the house of Israel. I am giving you a sign to take to these people. If you carry my sign and no one heeds it, they will be the worse for it, but you at least will be saved. If, on the other hand, you refuse to carry it and people do not get the message that I am sending to them, I am going to take out their punishment on you."

Ezekiel is asked to do a strange thing. He is to enact a kind of pantomime of the Babylonian exile. He is told by God to dress himself up like an exile, put an exile's baggage upon his shoulders, and go out through the city walls in the darkness of night, as one going sadly under great burden into captivity. In this way Ezekiel himself becomes a sign. He portrays a humiliated, captive people who have turned their backs upon their God and must suffer the consequence of being uprooted and driven out from the comfort and safety God has given them. Ezekiel, with his exile's clothing and baggage, was God's message. He symbolized in his own being what God was saying to the people. He was not told to stand on the corner and preach this message. He was not asked to write and publish it. He had to leave his own home for a time, pack his belongings and put them on his back, dig through the city wall, and go out into the blackness of night—"for I have made you," said God, "a sign for the house of Israel."

Let us substitute the color of blackness for the exile's clothing and for the baggage that Ezekiel carried by God's command. Certainly colors are used in all human societies as signs or symbols. From the most ancient and primitive people to our modern society, colors have been understood to convey powerful messages. The color symbolism of white Western societies has come, of course, to dominate most of the world. Wherever the white man has gone, his color symbolism—the assignment he has given to certain colors—has tended to become standard.

A simple example is the meaning of traffic signals. No matter where you are—in Hong Kong, Dar es Salaam, Santiago, or Atlanta—red means danger, yellow means caution, green means go. What about black and white? There is some ambiguity about these colors. But generally speaking, European and American painting, literature, and cultural artifacts have conveyed the message that white symbolizes truth, beauty, purity, and goodness, while black symbolizes shame, impurity, ignorance, and evil.

Western symbolism—carried around the world by Western armies and missionaries—has made people believe that God himself decreed that "white is right, brown can stick around, but black must go back." More than that, according to this symbolism, God is white and Satan is black.

Did God authorize this symbolism? Of course not. Nor did black people authorize it. White men, by the sheer power of their culture—their money, guns, and Bibles—made this kind of white/black symbolism operative first in Europe and America, later in South Africa, and now all over the world. But just as the white man can make up his mind about the meaning of blackness and back it up by his interpretation of the will of God, we black people can change that meaning.

This is no idle matter. Colors convey powerful religious meanings, as the history of liturgics shows. And if a white preacher like the Reverend Buchner Payne can say that God chose whiteness because there is no darkness in him and there can be no darkness in heaven, a black preacher can say that God chose blackness because God is mystery and cosmic fecundity, for there can be no white, lifeless sterility in heaven!

What I am really saying is that we black people have a right, even a responsibility, to interpret the Christian faith in such a way as to make blackness a profound expression of our religious experience. Even though black experience has usually been betrayal, suffering, and affliction, we can read the meaning of that experience in positive rather than negative terms, because of what we know about God and his relationship to those who trust him.

One day men came and reported to Jesus about some Galileans who had fallen into Pilate's hands and had been killed. Luke does not tell us the questions they asked, but they probably pertained to whether Jesus thought this tragic event demonstrated the sinfulness of the victims. In other words, was this God's punishment for their sins? "No," said Jesus, "but the same thing could happen to you if you do not repent of yours!" On another occasion when the disciples passed by a man born blind they asked, "Rabbi, who sinned, this man or his parents, that he was born blind?" Jesus answered, "It was not that this man sinned, or his parents, but that the works of God might be made manifest in him."

The implication of both of these incidents is that God permits tragedy and hardships to come upon us for mysterious reasons of his own, not necessarily because we are offenders more than others. Indeed, he may even command some people to bear greater burden than others in order that his will may be known. He summoned Ezekiel to bear the symbol of exile and captivity and sent him out into the darkness as a sign of what had been prepared for a rebellious people. While the false prophets lied about how much God was going to bless the people, Ezekiel dramatically portrayed the grim reality of their real situation.

Is there a lesson for us in Ezekiel's prophetic assignment? I believe so. In the face of man's false sense of security, in the face of his illusions about whom he is and what he is able to accomplish by his own hands, in the face of his lies about truth and justice, blackness and the black experience of suffering and oppression stand as God's witness to reality to the truth about life. Blackness is the way life really is. It is a sign of affliction and oppression, not of punishment and corruption. And there is a vast difference between the two that requires a complete revision of the color symbolism of Western culture. Blackness is indeed a symbol of what we have suffered, but we may bear it proudly, not only because we have learned how to survive and sing the songs of Zion in a strange land, but because, like Ezekiel, God has called us in our blackness to bear a message to all people.

In *The Gift of Black Folk*, W. E. B. Du Bois speaks of the black presence in America as tragedy reflected in the sorrow songs or spirituals, but he saw in the black experience something that said a great deal about the vulnerability of all human existence, about the elemental nature of suffering and woe, about death as a natural and inevitable part of life. This is the message of blackness assigned by God himself. In a civilization that believes all men can be sexually attractive and all women can be queen every day, in a culture where people hide from suffering and avert their eyes from the slums when they drive over them on thruways to suburbia, in a world that believes man is the measure of all things and human progress is inevitable, blackness is a religious symbol of a stern reality that continues to frustrate man's noblest designs, a reality that must be lived and experienced lest a people perish by their own fatuous illusions. The psalmist writes:

Thou dost sweep men away . . .
    like grass which is renewed in the morning:
in the morning it flourishes and is renewed;
    in the evening it fades and withers. . . .
For all our days pass away under thy wrath,
    our years come to end like a sigh.

Black people have always well understood those words. It is because of this understanding that we have learned to act like men and women of flesh and blood and to let only God be God. Like Paul we know how to be full and how to be empty. We know we live in a sinful, imperfect world and that emptiness is the portion given, soon or late, to all people. When we cry out in the midnight hour, "O Lord, have mercy on my soul," it is because we know that life "ain't been no crystal stair" and "the higher you climb the harder you fall." God made life that way, and man can never change it.

Blackness is a beautiful sensitivity to the hard, tragic dimension in life—a part of living that everyone must learn to negotiate, because, whether rich or poor, famous or infamous, black or white, we are all pitiable, vulnerable human beings and we have to go down into the pit together. Blackness is a message to the world that a man's arm is too short to box with God; that he is so high you can't get over him, so low you can't get under him, so wide you can't get around him— you must come in by the Door. And that Door is the door of trials and tribulations that is personified by Jesus. That Door is what makes a people both humble and strong. "Yet do I marvel at this curious thing: to make a poet black, and bid him sing."

I have been talking about blackness as a symbol of perennial human condition. Blackness is also the message that man must struggle against every power that seeks to subdue and dehumanize him. Blackness symbolizes the truth that even though you may be down, you are not necessarily out and by God's grace you will rise again.

Jesus Christ is crucial to black Christianity because darkness was his experience, and we know something about darkness. The Good Friday spiritual asks the question, "Were you there?" And the unspoken answer is, "Yes, we were all there when the Nigger of Galilee was lynched in Jerusalem." Is there any wonder that we can identify with him?

Black people, whether in America or in Africa, know Jesus as the Oppressed Man of God, who fraternized with harlots and sinners, who helped the poor and lowly, who struggled against the powers of evil in church and state, who was crucified in apparent defeat. We, of all the people of the world, can identify with that story because that is precisely what blackness has meant for us—lowliness, struggle, and defeat. Like Jesus on the cross, we too have cried out against the darkness in our flesh and in our environment, "My God, my God, why have you forsaken us?"

But as Jesus stood the test, we too stood the test, singing our blues and gospel, finger-popping all the while. As his strength was made perfect in weakness, so was ours. We never stopped struggling against the powers of oppression, poverty, and racism, and I believe we never will, because we have learned from Jesus that life itself is a struggle, and if you can't stand the heat, you will never be able to work in the kitchen. "In the world you have tribulation; but be of good cheer, I have overcome the world."

Blackness, therefore, is God's message through us to all people that to resist, to struggle, to wrestle, fight, and pray—and yet laugh and sing and "get happy"—is what it means to be a human being. Human beings know how to love and have compassion and get along with people in this world.

We do indeed have enemies and we have by no means conquered them within or without. But we continue to struggle with hope because we believe that even in death we shall be victorious through the Oppressed Son of God who conquered death, even death on the cross. That is why, as strange as it may sound in a world dominated by Western symbolism, we can speak of Jesus as our Black Messiah, because in so doing we chain ourselves not only to his cross but to his resurrection from defeat; we make blackness the sign and symbol not only of his struggle but also of his glorious victory which we will share.

My final word is that we have little choice but to be God's sign and live, or refuse to be God's sign and die as a people. We did not ask to be born in this color, nor did we choose the slavery, suffering, and humiliation against which we have been struggling all these years. But neither did Ezekiel have a choice when God called him in Tel-abib to bear witness to the meaning of the Babylonian captivity. The only choice he had, or that we have, is how we shall interpret the meaning of our individual and corporate lives. Only a religious meaning, only a religious interpretation of our pilgrimage, can satisfy the deepest yearnings of our hearts.

How, then, shall we understand blackness? As an accident of history in a world of absurdity and meaninglessness? As a curse and a punishment? Or as a profound and mysterious assignment from God by which we have been called to bear witness to the message of his judgment and his grace to all the nations of the world and especially to white America?

In a nation where blackness and oppression have seemed inseparable, my faith will permit no other answer than God has made my people a sign to an arrogant, self-aggrandizing, rebellious generation. He has commanded us to say to the world: "This is your life too. This is what it means to be human—to suffer, to struggle, to fight with hope against the powers of hell—to die and to be raised victorious with Jesus Christ. Therefore, take heed of us and live!"

It is the responsibility of the black church to preserve this black image of humanity against all the whitenizing acids of the modern age. Young black men and women of this generation, do not forsake the rock from which you were hewn to choose an easier but less challenging road on which to travel. Give your heart, mind, and will to God. Return to the black church and reality, to humanity and struggle, to the assignment of your blackness. For God has not left himself without a witness in this evil day. As he said to the prophet Ezekiel, so he continues to say, "Son of man, you dwell in the midst of a rebellious house. . . . Therefore, . . . prepare for yourself an exile's baggage, . . . for I have made you a sign for the house of Israel." God has made us a sign of judgment, grace, and love. Let all who have eyes to see, see and believe in the struggle and the victory through Jesus Christ, our crucified and risen Lord.